Eating Well in Wisconsin

Jerry Minnich's Guide to
Eating Well in Wisconsin

PRAIRIE OAK PRESS

Madison, Wisconsin

Prairie Oak Press
2577 University Avenue
Madison, Wisconsin 53705

Cover design by Flying Fish Graphics, Blue Mounds, Wisconsin
Title page photo by Brent Nicastro
Typeset by KC Graphics, Inc., Madison, Wisconsin
Printed in the United States of America by BookCrafters, Chelsea, Michigan

Library of Congress Cataloging-in-Publication Data

Minnich, Jerry
        Jerry Minnich's guide to eating well in Wisconsin / Jerry Minnich.
— 1st ed.
        p. cm.
        ISBN 1-879483-15-7 : $8.95
        1. Restaurants—Wisconsin—Guidebooks. 2. Wisconsin—Guidebooks.
I. Title. II. Title: Eating well in Wisconsin
TX907.3.W6M56 1993
647.95775—dc20   93-31125
                                                        CIP

Introduction

This is a guide to eating well in Wisconsin. Note that I have not used the term "dining" in the title. This is intentional. Not that you cannot find excellent dining establishments in Wisconsin, and dine in them to your heart and stomach's content. You certainly can, and I have identified many of those establishments in this guide. But Wisconsin is a Midwestern state, after all, and most people go about eating and dining in a more casual way than people do in, say, California or New York. Many of the restaurants I recommend in this book are trés casual. If you come in wearing a tie, the other customers may look at you strangely. And if you say you came to "dine," they might even get a little nervous. But, then, there are restaurants where you have to wear a tie, most of the entrees have French names, and some guy with a tux will come up to you and say, "My name is Bruce and I will be your waiter tonight." The point is, there are both "dining establishments" and "eating places" in Wisconsin, and I did not want to restrict my guide to either of them. You can eat well in both.

This is not a critical guide, except that I have tried to identify the state's truly outstanding restaurants. Rather, it is a ready source of information about good places to eat in Wisconsin. Every restaurant I list in this book is a restaurant I recommend. Because a restaurant is not listed in this guide certainly does not mean that it is not a good restaurant—simply that I have yet to learn about it. If you know a restaurant that should be included in the next edition of this guide, I would greatly appreciate your telling me about it. Just send a short note to me, and a menu, if possible, at the address on the back of this book.

The three-star (***) designation identifies what are, in my estimation, the outstanding restaurants in Wisconsin. Not all of them are "dining establishments" and not all are expensive. But most are, admittedly, both. But there are also some inexpensive three-star restaurants, including one hamburger parlor and one Italian restaurant where the average dinner is seven dollars and you might not get a glass with your bottle of beer unless you ask for it. These restaurants are included because, in my opinion, they do what they do better than anyone else. I appreciate a world-class hamburger far more than a mediocre chateaubriand. (But, then, I appreciate a world-class chateaubriand far more than a mediocre hamburger, too.) Awarding stars, or diamonds, or forks, is always a dangerous thing to do, arbitrary as it is, and subject as it is to restaurants' sudden changing, and restaurant staffs having occasional off-nights, as they do. Despite the inherent perils, I have decided to go ahead with the star system because I think it will be a genuine service to the reader, especially one who is unfamiliar with most of these restaurants. Again, if you think that a great restaurant has been overlooked, please let me know.

Virtually no chain restaurants are included in this guide. This is not because I am snobbish, but because I figure you already know what the food is like in most chain restaurants—their chief asset is their consistency, after all—and you have your likes and dislikes among them. Rather, I have spent my energies in attempting to lead you to good restaurants that you might not otherwise know about.

No restaurant has paid a fee of any kind to be included in this guide, nor have I ever asked for or accepted such a fee. Any gift certificates I have received from well-meaning restaurateurs have gone unused. This is an independent guide, subjective to be sure, but at least unbiased in this regard.

The Supper Club and the Fish Fry

For those of you who are new to Wisconsin, I must explain two ubiquitous state institutions. One is the supper club, the other is the fish fry. Neither is exclusive to the state—you'll find both in other parts of the Midwest—but newcomers often wonder about them, as I did when I arrived here from New Jersey, many years ago, and so I'll try to elucidate.

A supper club in some parts of the country is synonymous with a nightclub—like the Stork Club, or the Rainbow Room, those places where Fred Astaire and Ginger Rogers and their friends dined and danced in tuxes and evening gowns in the late '30s. Not so in Wisconsin. Here, it is an old-time restaurant, rapidly falling out of style in the larger cities but still very popular in smaller towns and rural areas. The supper club is usually fairly large and comfortable. It has a bar, usually separate from the dining room. The most popular entrees are steaks, deep-fat-fried freshwater fish and seafood (especially shrimp), baked chicken, and pork chops. Sometimes beef liver. Baked potatoes (often in aluminum foil jackets) and hash browns are common. Cooked vegetables are seldom on the menu. In former times, each table received a relish tray, typically containing radishes, celery and carrot sticks, three-bean salad, scallions, pickled beets, and cottage cheese. More and more, the relish tray is being replaced by the salad bar. There are always daily specials. On Sunday the special is always chicken. On Saturday night the special is prime rib (you can count on it). And on Friday night the special—without a doubt—is a fish fry. Usually the fish is ocean or lake perch, walleyed pike, or cod (the last is now sometimes steamed, but that is very untraditional, a concession to today's lighter eating habits). French fries or hash browns, and coleslaw, always accompany the fried fish, and often it is an all-you-can-eat affair.

If I seem to denigrate the fish fry, I do not mean to. I am a devotee. I cannot count the number of Wisconsin supper-club fish fries I have enjoyed in the past several decades. I still enjoy them.

Why the fish fry? I don't know the origins of the custom, and I haven't met anyone who does. I suppose it might have to do with the state's large

Catholic population (meatless Fridays) or the Great Lakes commercial fishing tradition, or the French voyageurs, or even the Native Americans, for all I know. I would appreciate any reliable information.

A "fish boil" is a different thing—except that it, too, amounts to eating fish on Friday night. The outdoor fish boil does trace its roots directly to the commercial Great Lakes fishing camps of old, when the cook would boil up a mess of fish for the whole crew. The boil is very popular in Door County, especially, where quite a ritual is made of it for the enjoyment of tourists. Lake Superior whitefish or lake trout is boiled with potatoes (and sometimes onions, carrots, and seasonings) in a huge, black, wood-fired kettle. When the water begins to boil, the "Master Boiler" throws a big cupful of kerosene on the fire, causing a large flareup which quickly boils the fat off the top of the boiling water and into the fire, all to the applause of admiring customers. Then the fish and vegetables are removed and served up with coleslaw, homemade breads, and cherry pie. It's one of Wisconsin's most treasured traditions.

One more warning, for those who like to drink a manhattan or an old fashioned before dinner. In Wisconsin, if you don't specify whiskey in these drinks, you will receive California brandy, instead. I don't know why.

Definitions and Abbreviations

Holiday hours. I have not noted holiday policies of the restaurants in this guide. Most restaurants are closed on Christmas and New Year's Day, and many close early on December 24th. Some close on Thanksgiving, while others specialize in Thanksgiving Day dinners. You will be wise to call any restaurant at which you hope to eat on a holiday, whether it be Christmas or the Fourth of July. Especially do not drive long distances to a restaurant on holidays without checking beforehand.

Wheelchair accessibility. The wheelchair-accessible ratings are based largely on owners' reports. I admit, I have not checked each of these more than 250 restaurants for the accuracy of those reports. Please tell me, if reality differs from these reports in any instance.

Smoking. When I say "Totally nonsmoking," I mean that smoking is not allowed anywhere inside the premises. Some restaurants ban smoking in dining areas but allow it in the cocktail lounge or bar. I do not consider that to be totally nonsmoking.

Alcohol. In the restaurant listings, when I say "Cocktail lounge/bar," that means that beer, wine, and liquor are served, at dining tables and also in a separate cocktail lounge or bar. In some cases, the bar might not be separate from the dining room. When I say "Full bar," I mean that beer, wine, and liquor are served, but only at dining tables. When I say "Beer and wine are served," I mean that they are served only at dining tables, and that no hard liquor is available. "No alcohol" means no beer, wine, or liquor is served.

"Catering service" means that the restaurant caters parties off the premises. "Private parties" means that the restaurant will host private gatherings in a separate room or rooms on the premises.

Children. When I say "Small children not encouraged," I mean that small children are not absolutely prohibited, but that the restaurant is really not suited to small children. It is a polite way of suggesting that you might take children to a more suitable restaurant. When I say "Children's portions," I mean that there is no children's menu, but that the management will accommodate children with smaller portions at reduced prices. Even when "Children's menu" is listed, most restaurants will serve children's portions of other items. Restaurants really do seek to please you. Don't be afraid to ask.

Vegetarian entrees. I have tried to identify those restaurants that are best for vegetarians. Some have primarily vegetarian menus. This, however, is a tricky business, as vegetarians know. Vegetable soups may be based in beef broth. Salads may come unannounced with hard-boiled eggs, cheese, or bacon bits. If you require a totally vegetarian meal—no matter what kind of a vegetarian you are—I strongly suggest that you call the restaurant beforehand, explain your needs very clearly, and be sure that the restaurant can fill those needs.

Credit card code. MC = MasterCard. VI = Visa. AE = American Express. Dis = Discover. DC = Diners Club. CB = Carte Blanche. In listings, "All major credit cards" means all of the above.

Checks. Most restaurants are very good about accepting checks. However, even if the listing says "Out-of-town checks OK with ID," it is best to clear this with your waiter before ordering. Policies do change—especially if the restaurant has been hit with a couple of bad checks in the week before you visit.

Wisconsin has many excellent restaurants and lots of good food, from the sour cherry pies of Door County to the Cornish pasties of Mineral Point, from Friday night catfish fries on the Great Mississippi to elegant dining on the shores of Lake Michigan. I hope that this little guidebook will help you to find some of these restaurants and these foods, and that you will return again and again for more of the same. And don't forget—if you happen upon a hidden restaurant treasure not listed in this book, don't keep it to yourself. Write to me right away.

Bon appétit! Good eatin'!

Please pass the tartar.

Jerry Minnich
September 21, 1993

Contents

Admiralty Room
The Edgewater Hotel
Continental / French
666 Wisconsin Ave., Madison / 608-256-9071
(At the end of Wisconsin Ave., on the shore of Lake Mendota)

The Admiralty Room is one of the most elegant restaurants in town, offering spectacular picture-window views of Lake Mendota, complete with dazzling sunsets and occasional dazzling storms. Since 1948, it has been a favorite Madison restaurant for special occasion dinners—the place where UW students take Mom and Dad, the place for anniversary celebrations, for special birthdays. The decor is sparkling, with crisp white linen, crystal goblets, fresh flowers, and candlelit tables, and the waiters are efficient and attentive without being obsequious. The menu features a wide variety of steaks, veal dishes, fresh fish, and poultry, most dishes prepared in the Continental style with some tableside preparations. There is an extensive wine list.

Expensive. Most dinners $15-30. Serving daily breakfast 7-10, lunch 11:30-2:30, dinner 5:30-10. Sun. brunch 11-2. Complimentary underground parking. Wheelchair accessible. Smoking & nonsmoking sections. Cocktail lounge/bar. Children's birthday parties. Children's menu. Reservations essential. Harp music Fri.-Sat. nights. Catering service. Private parties (max. 800). MC, VI, AE, DC, CB. Out-of-town checks OK with ID.

Aliota's on East Washington
Continental / Italian
3710 E. Washington Ave., Madison / 608-241-7900
(Corner of Hwy. 151, inside the Midway Hotel)

Yes, this Aliota's is run by members of the same family that has operated the famous Aliota's in Milwaukee for more than forty years. And, fortunately for Madison diners, the family brought the recipes with them—especially the one for minestrone, which is the best in town. There is a full Italian menu here, with more than forty entrees, but the restaurant is perhaps best known for its spiedini, Italian breaded steaks, homemade ravioli, veal dishes, and pasta.

Moderate. Most dinners $10-13. Serving Sun. 4-10, Mon.-Thurs. 11-10, Fri. 11-11. Sat. 4-11. Parking lot. Wheelchair accessible. Smoking & nonsmoking sections. Cocktail lounge/bar. Children's menu. Seniors discount (age 55+). Reservations recommended (essential on Fri.-Sat. nights). Takeouts. Piano bar Fri.-Sat. nights. Catering service. Private parties (max. 200). MC, VI, AE, Dis, DC. Out-of-town checks OK with ID.

Antonio's
Italian
1109 S. Park St., Madison / 608-251-1412

Antonio's, founded in 1986, is one of Madison's premier Italian restaurants, operated by Rose Marie and Tony Schiavo, whose family has been running taverns and restaurants in Madison for several generations. There are at least twenty different pasta entrees here, but perhaps the specialty of the house is spiedini— tender rolled sirloin stuffed with a moist Italian dressing , then breaded and broiled. Incomparable! The atmosphere is casual at Antonio's, and the cooking is comfortably home-style. All in all, this is a very pleasant place to come for a relaxed and excellent meal. Highly recommended.

Inexpensive to moderate. Most dinners $7-17. Serving Tues.-Sat. 4-9. Parking lot. Wheelchair accessible. Smoking & nonsmoking sections. Cocktail lounge/bar. Children's menu. Reservations recommended. Takeouts. Catering service. Private parties (max. 80). MC, VI, AE. No checks.

Bahn Thai
Thai
2809 University Ave., Madison / 608-233-3900
944 Williamson St., Madison / 608-256-0202

Bahn Thai was the first Thai restaurant in Madison, and it is still the most popular. There are now two restaurants with this name—one on the near-west side, a newer and more spacious one on the near-east side—and they now have different owners. No matter, both serve authentic Thai dishes, ranging from mild to very hot in spice. (Be sure to express your preference when ordering.) A typical dish is Masaman Nur, with beef, potatoes, peanuts, and onions in a mild red curry of coconut milk, coriander, cumin, cinnamon, and anise. There are several stir-fries and noodle dishes, including the popular pad Thai, with rice noodles, pork, shrimp, tofu, and bamboo shoots, topped with chopped scallions and peanuts. The winning aspect of Thai cooking is the artful merging of exciting spices and the use of peanuts, coconut milk, lemon grass, peppers, and seafood. The two Bahn Thais are good representatives of this cuisine in Madison.

Inexpensive. Most dinners $5-8. *University Ave.* serving Sun. noon-10, Mon.-Sat. 11-10. *Williamson St.* serving Sun. 5-10, Mon.-Sat. 11-10. Parking lot. Wheelchair accessible. *University Ave.* totally nonsmoking. *Williamson St..* smoking & nonsmoking sections. Full bar. Reservations recommended. Local deliveries. Takeouts. Catering service. MC, VI, AE, DC. Out-of-town checks OK with ID.

Bailiwick's—An American Eatery
American
6619 Odana Rd., Madison / 608-833-0110

This elegant restaurant, located at the Radisson Inn, serves distinctive American cuisine from five distinct regions: the Great Midwest, Northeast, South, Southwest, and Pacific Northwest. No matter from which part of the U.S. you come, you can find a touch of home at Bailiwick's.

Inexpensive to moderate. Most dinners $6-15. Serving Sun. 7-10, 10-2 (brunch), 5-10, weekdays 6:30-2, 5-10, Fri.-Sat. dinner until 10:30. Parking lot. Wheelchair accessible. Smoking & nonsmoking sections. Cocktail lounge. Reservations recommended. Private parties (max. 30). All major credit cards. No checks.

★ ★ ★
Blue Marlin
Seafood
101 N. Hamilton St., Madison / 608-255-2255
(Right across the street from the Capitol)

In a delightful setting, housed in an 1850-circa building, the Blue Marlin serves exquisite fresh fish and seafood dishes, the menu changing often with the most attractive catch of the day. Some specialties of the house include seafood linguini, grilled lobster, and, of course, blue marlin. Many restaurants serve fish, but few know how to prepare it right. Here, fish is everything, and head chef (and co-owner) Henry Doane certainly prepares it right. He uses no cream in sauces, but instead yogurt, homemade mayonnaise, compound butters, vinaigrettes, and olive oil, keeping saturated fat to a minimum. Most of the fish is grilled simply, and is accented with spices and compound butters. There is a classic San Francisco fish stew and a most unusual entree, a filet mignon stuffed with fresh oysters, called Australian carpetbag steak. Everything at the Blue Marlin, from the entree to the fresh salads, to the desserts, is done with exquisite care and attention to detail, making this one of the best restaurants in the state.

Expensive. Most dinners $17-27. Serving Tues.-Fri. 11:30-2:30 & 5:30-10, Sat. & Sun. 5:30-10. Closed Mon. Nearby public parking. Wheelchair accessible. Totally nonsmoking. Full bar. Small children not encouraged. Reservations strongly recommended. MC, VI, AE, DC. No checks.

Botticelli's
Italian / American
107 King St., Madison / 608-257-1110

Botticelli's, opened in 1991, is a popular Capitol-area restaurant specializing in creative Italian cuisine and great bakery items. Some of the specialties include fettucine Alfredo with vegetables, spaghetti carbonara, marinated grilled chicken breast, vegetarian antipasto, poached whitefish, and rosemary chicken. There are also individual pizzas and great desserts. Botticelli's is very popular at lunch, surrounded as it is by office buildings, and also for breakfast and weekend brunch. It has just the right formula for success in Madison's downtown area.

Inexpensive to moderate. Most dinners $6-12. Serving Mon.-Fri. 7 am-10 pm, Sat. & Sun. 8 am-10 pm. Nearby public parking ramp. Wheelchair accessible. Totally nonsmoking until 5 pm; limited smoking area after 5 pm. Full bar. Children's portions. Reservations recommended. Takeouts. MC, VI. Out-of-town checks OK with ID.

Canterbury Coffeehouse
American cafe
315 W. Gorham St., Madison / 608-258-9911
(In the campus area just off State St.)

Established in 1991, Canterbury is at once a charming bookstore, a restaurant for light vegetarian brunches, lunches, and dinners, and—since 1993—an inn where overnight guests might repose in literary surroundings. Entrees include pasta salads, a hummus platter, Greek salad, fruit salad, and vegetarian chili. There are some wonderful desserts, including "chocolate surrender cheesecake," hazelnut cappuccino torte, caramel apple granny pie, and ice cream specialties. Designer coffees and teas round out the menu. All are served on colorful Italian painted pottery, adding to the charm. Far from rushing patrons through their meals or snacks, the management encourages them to linger, to read a book or perhaps play a game of chess (board and chesspersons provided).

Inexpensive. Most entrees $5-7. Serving Sun.-Thurs. 10 am-10:45 pm, Fri. 10 am-11:45 pm, Sat. 9 am-11:45 pm. Nearby public parking lots. Wheelchair accessible. Totally nonsmoking. No alcohol. Reservations not needed, except for parties of 6 or more. Takeouts. Varied live entertainment several nights a week, including jazz, folk, and classical music. Occasional theater performances. Private parties (max. 12). MC, VI. Out-of-town checks OK with ID.

Casa de Lara
Mexican
341 State St., Madison / 608-251-7200
(Corner of State & Gorham Sts., between the campus and the Capitol)

Casa de Lara is Madison's upscale Mexican restaurant. It serves Mexican cuisine rather than the computer-driven tacos and burritos found at chain versions of Mexican restaurants. In a slick, urban, second-floor setting, using Mexican artifacts for deoration, this restaurant presents superb and authentic Mexican dishes, using cactus, mole, various chilis, and traditional herbs and spices. *Especialidades de la casa* include Nopalito Con Queso—chicken and shrimp sauteed with cactus and onions, simmered in ancho and pasilla red sauce. Chayotes Rellenos is made from a vegetable pear indigenous to Mexico, filled with meat, green onions, tomatoes, and spices, and topped with two kinds of cheese. Mole, of course, is the Mexican sauce made from various ingredients, here from unsweetened chocolate, pumpkin seeds, nuts, cinnamon, and five different kinds of peppers. There are four different mole dishes, the most popular served with chicken. Of course, there are tacos, enchiladas, chimichangas, burritos, and fajitas, all exceeding the usual American versions of these items. Casa de Lara is the best representative of true Mexican cooking in Madison, perhaps in all of Wisconsin.

Moderate. Most dinners $9-13. Serving Mon.-Thurs. 11-10, Fri. & Sat. 11-11. Nearby public parking lot. Not wheelchair accessible. Smoking & nonsmoking sections. Full bar. Children's portions. Reservations accepted. Takeouts. Catering service. Live Mexican folk music Sat. eve. MC, VI, AE, DC. No checks.

China House
Chinese
1256 S. Park St., Madison / 608-257-1079
(1 mi N of Hwys. 12/18, on the W side of Park St.)

There are many Chinese restaurants in Madison, but this is definitely one of the best, for a varied menu, well-prepared fresh foods, and consistent quality. The decor is authentic, and is enhanced by fresh flowers and candle-lit tables. House specialites include hot and sour soup, pot stickers, cold noodles with sesame sauce, clergyman chicken, Hunan lamb, two-delicacy scallops, crisp and spicy shrimp, whole lobster, and crispy whole fish. There are specialties in the Hunan, Szechuan, Cantonese, and Peking styles. In more than twenty years, I have never had an unsatisfactory experience at China House.

Inexpensive. Most dinners $6-10. Serving from lunch menu daily 11:30-3. Serving from dinner menu Sun.-Thurs. 11:30-10, Fri.-Sat. 11:30-11. Parking lot. Wheelchair accessible. Smoking & nonsmoking sections. Cocktail lounge/bar. Small children not encouraged. Reservations recommended. Local deliveries. Takeouts. Private parties (max. 35). MC, VI, AE, DC, CB. Out-of-town checks OK with ID.

Crandall's at the Depot
American
640 W. Washington Ave., Madison
(6 blocks W of the Capitol, at the railroad tracks)

On the day that this book was going to press, word arrived that Crandall's at the Depot was folding its menu forever, and that a new restaurant would take its place in a few weeks. This was sad news, indeed, to the many Madisonians who had treasured Crandall's since its inception in 1946, first in its Capitol square location, then, beginning in 1990, in the old train station. Crandall's was honored each year, in several reader polls, for having the best Friday night fish fry in town. My first impulse was to remove the restaurant from this book—but then I reconsidered. Despite the change in ownership and style, the restaurant will still occupy one of the best spots in downtown Madison, and will still have an urbane cocktail lounge with art deco touches. The dining room is located in the former passenger waiting room of the depot. It is a grand space, and I hope it will serve well in the future. Next to the restaurant is a vintage train with the cars serving as retail shops. Between the train cars and the depot is a small, pleasant, outdoor dining area. Although personally saddened to see Crandall's go (I had been a patron for 28 years), I look for good times in the future at this prime location. (The last vestige of Crandall's now left in Madison is Crandall's Carryout & Catering, located on the west side at 6401 University Avenue.)

David's Restaurant
American
909 E. Broadway, Madison / 608-222-0048

This unassuming roadhouse, located next to a bait shop between Highway 51 and Monona Drive, is one of the true surprises of the Madison restaurant scene. Owner and chef David Scheifel honed his skills in some of the best upscale eateries in Madison and elsewhere, and now exercises his creative talents in his own kitchen. The results are truly impressive, especially (in the author's opinion) the Tuesday night pot roast. David turns out quality regional dishes, using real in-house stocks, soups, and sauces, all served in a very relaxed atmosphere at bargain prices. This is one of the best dinner values in town, highly recommended.

Inexpensive to moderate. Most dinners $6-14. Serving dinner Tues.-Sat. 5:30-9. Fri. fish fry from 5 pm. Closed Sun.-Mon. Parking lot. Wheelchair accessible. No policy on smoking. Bar room. Reservations recommended. Takeouts. No credit cards. Out-of-town checks OK with ID.

★ ★ ★
Dotty Dumpling's Dowry
American
116 N. Fairchild St., Madison / 608-255-3175
(Just off State St., near the Capitol)

Dotty's, which calls itself, tongue in cheek, "World Hamburger Headquarters," is close to fulfilling its own prophecy. Dotty's hamburgers have achieved, if not worldwide fame, at least national renown. Annual winner of "best hamburger in Madison" awards (no other restaurant ever comes close), Dotty's has also been featured in *Midwest Living* magazine, in *USA Today*, and in other widely circulated periodicals and guidebooks. The burgers here, with a wide choice of toppings, are indeed likely to be the best you've ever tasted. But there is more—

much more. Dotty's also has the best French fries in town, the best chili (two varieties—hot and super-hot), an incomparable Italian sausage sandwich with marinated peppers, a dynamite chicken sandwich, genuine malted milk shakes, and the best homemade pies in this or any other town. With so many culinary superlatives to its credit, we can't help but name this hamburger bar one of the best restaurants in the state. You'll also love the eclectic and decidedly whimsical decor, featuring toys, sports artifacts, stuffed animals, posters, and prints from the 1930s and '40s. Dotty's is a Madison institution, a fun place to be and a very fine restaurant.

Inexpensive. Most dinners under $10. Serving Sun. noon-8:30, Mon.-Wed. 11-10, Thurs.-Sat. 11 a.m.-midnight. Nearby public parking ramp. Wheelchair accessible. Smoking & nonsmoking sections. Domestic & imported beers on tap. Reservations not accepted. Takeouts. Live jazz band Thurs. night. MC, VI. No checks.

El Charro
Mexican
600 Williamson St., Madison / 608-255-1828
(In the Gateway mall, at W end of Williamson St.)

What began as a food cart on the Capitol square eventually grew into a very popular family restaurant on Madison's near-east side. El Charro is owned and run by the Avila family. It serves up wonderful fajitas, enchiladas, tamales, tacos, tostadas, burritos, quesadillas, flautas, chile rellenos, and more. You can get a great Mexican breakfast here, including huevos rancheros, and inexpensive take-out items a la carte. The service is quick and friendly, and the check will be a pleasant surprise.

Inexpensive. Most dinners $4-6. Serving Mon.-Fri. 11-9, Sat. 8 a.m.-9 p.m., Sun. 8:30-3. (Closed Sun. in summer.) Parking lot. Wheelchair accessible. No smoking policy (but there is little of it). Full bar.

Ella's Deli & Ice Cream Parlor
American / Kosher
2902 E. Washington Ave., Madison / 608-241-5291
(3 mi E of the Capitol on Hwy. 151)

This is the best children's restaurant in Madison, a tremendous favorite with families and a great place to take visitors. There are more than 50 animated displays inside—cartoon characters, clowns, sky flyers, antique video boxes, tightrope cyclers, etc.—as well as an authentic 1927 full-size carousel that gives rides to both children and adults. With all the activity, the restaurant surprisingly is not all that noisy, even when it is full—which it often is. A definite bonus for adults is that the food is genuinely good. The menu has as many pages as some best-selling novels, and includes Kosher meats, wonderful cabbage soup, good Jewish rye, eggs and omelets, hot dogs, tuna melts, lox, bagels, chopped liver, and other things to keep everybody happy. There are 24 flavors of ice cream, and—need we say?—an outstanding dessert menu. My personal favorite is the grilled pound cake, served warm with French vanilla ice cream, hot fudge, and whipped cream. Worry about dieting tomorrow.

Inexpensive. Most dinners $4-6. Serving Sun.-Thurs. 10 am-11 pm, Fri.-Sat. 10 am-midnight. Parking lot. Wheelchair accessible. Smoking & nonsmoking sections. No alcohol. Children's menu. Children's birthday parties a specialty. Reservations not accepted. Takeouts. MC, VI. Out-of-town checks OK with ID.

Essen Haus
German
514 E. Wilson St., Madison / 608-255-4674
(Several blocks E of Capitol Square)

This is the place to go in Madison for hearty German food. And it is definitely the place to go if you are a beer aficionado. With 16 German beers on draft and more than 280 bottled beers from around the world, the Essen Haus is truly a beer-lover's paradise. Sauerbraten, weiner schnitzel, potato dumplings, rouladen, liver-dumpling soup, and other traditional German specialties are all on the menu, here, along with prime rib and other American dishes. The atmosphere is designed for fun.

Moderate. Most dinners $9-11. Serving Sun. 3-10, Tues.-Thurs. 5-10, Fri.-Sat. 5-11. Closed Mon. Parking lot. Wheelchair accessible. Smoking & nonsmoking sections. Cocktail lounge/bar. Children's birthday parties. Children's menu. Reservations recommended. Nightly dancing to live polka music. Local deliveries. Catering service. MC, VI. Out-of-town checks OK with ID.

The Fess Restaurant
Continental / French
123 E. Doty St., Madison / 608-256-0263
(Just a block from the Capitol)

The Fess is one of the most popular restaurants in Madison. Located in an 1848 hotel, now a National Historic Landmark, it has been pleasing diners since 1975. The atmosphere is one of Victorian elegance, with crisp, white linen, period lighting fixtures, sparkling crystal, and potted palms. In addition to the main dining room, there are several small, intimate rooms. The two bars are popular ones with the crowd from the Capitol, which is only a block away. In summer, the Fess outdoor garden, seating 150, is perhaps the most desirable dining space in town. Fess specialties include grilled lamb en brochette, Coquille St. Jacques Parisienne, and filet mignon au poivre. There are fresh seafood specialties nightly, and excellent desserts, all made right in the Fess' own bakery. The Sunday brunch here is also one of the most popular in town, summer or winter. Despite the excellent food and the elegant surroundings, prices at the Fess are surprisingly modest.

Moderate. Most dinners $9-17. Serving Mon.-Fri. 11:30-2 & 5-9:45. Sat.-Sun. brunch 10:30-2:30, dinner 5-9:45. Public parking ramp contiguous with hotel. Wheelchair accessible. Smoking & nonsmoking sections. Two cocktail lounges. Children's birthday parties. Children's portions. Reservations recommended. Catering service. Private parties (max. 150). All major credit cards. Checks OK with ID.

Francie's Casual Cafe
American
2424 University Ave., Madison / 608-233-4080

Francie's is located in the Best Western/InnTowner, one block south of the University Hospitals and Clinics. The dining room is cheerfully and abundantly appointed with green plants, and there is plenty of light from the skylights and large windows facing the street and small outdoor terrace. Specialties include steak Diane and a chicken stir-fry, large salads, and some of the best clam chowder in Wisconsin. The Friday night fish fry is popular, as is the Sunday brunch-buffet.

Inexpensive to moderate. Most dinners $8-16. Serving Mon.-Sat. 6:30-2 & 5-10, Sun. 6:30-2 & 5-9 (brunch 10-2). Parking lot. Wheelchair accessible. Smoking & nonsmoking sections. Cocktail lounge. Children's birthday parties. Children's menu. Seniors discount (55). Reservations recommended. Takeouts. Catering service. Private parties (max. 250). All major credit cards. Checks OK with Telecheck approval.

Ginza of Tokyo
Japanese / Steakhouse
6734 Odana Rd., Madison / 608-833-8282
(1 blk E of West Towne shopping mall)

Here is Japanese food with heft and spirit. Chicken teriyaki, hibachi sirloin, hibachi scallops, tempura, sukiyaki, and, yes, sushi are all featured at this popular west-side spot. Hibachi items are cooked and served before your eyes at the hibachi table, which is manned by some very talented and entertaining knife-handlers. Of course, traditional Japanese dinners are also served. There is a sushi bar and private tea rooms for intimate dinners.

Moderate. Most dinners $9-14. Serving Sun. 4:30-9, weekdays 5-10, Fri. 5-11, Sat. 4:30-11. Parking lot. Wheelchair accessible. Smoking & nonsmoking sections. Full bar. Children's menu. Reservations essential. Takeouts. Catering service. Private tea rooms. MC, VI, AE, DC.

Goeden's Seafood Restaurant
Seafood / Oyster bar
529 University Ave., Madison / 608-256-1991
(Corner of Frances St., at the UW campus)

Goeden's is the oldest continually operating seafood restaurant in Madison, founded in 1922 and still run by the original Goeden family. A University of Wisconsin campus institution for generations, it offers visitors a genuine nautical atmosphere, such as might be found in coastal regions of the U.S. It also has Madison's only true raw bar, serving both drinks and raw oysters, boiled shrimp, and barbequed spiced shrimp. The menu offers a variety of seafood, both grilled and fried. For truly good fish and seafood, well-prepared and served at modest prices, Goeden's is highly recommended.

Inexpensive. Most dinners $5-10. Serving Sun. 3-8, Mon.-Thurs. 11-8:45, Fri.-Sat. 11-10. Parking lot. Wheelchair accessible. Smoking & nonsmoking sections. Cocktail lounge/bar (limited hours). Children's portions on request. Reservations not accepted. Local deliveries. Takeouts. No credit cards. Local checks OK with ID.

The Highland Grille
American / Supper club
7475 Mineral Point Rd., Madison / 608-833-7911

Old-time Madison residents will certainly remember Rhode's, on West Main Street, near the railroad tracks. Rhode's eventually moved far west, to the upscale High Point Center, and then, in 1992, became the Highland Grille, under the new ownership of Don Arenander. But those old-time residents will be happy to know that the Highland has maintained the same high standards that made Rhode's a perennial favorite with Madison families. The decor is light and airy, with sky-lights and lots of potted plants and trees. Walleyed pike, shrimp, fettucine Alfredo, steaks, and barbequed ribs still dominate the menu. And, yes, the navy bean soup is still outstanding and the service is still attentive and friendly. Look for the restaurant among the other establishments, in the shopping mall. It's just west of West Towne Mall.

Inexpensive to moderate. Most dinners $7-16. Serving Mon.-Tues. 11-9, Wed.-Thurs. 11-9:30, Fri. 11-10:30, Sat. 4-10. Sun. brunch 9-2, dinner 2-9. Off-street parking. Wheelchair accessible. Smoking & nonsmoking sections. Cocktail lounge. Children's birthday parties. Children's menu. Reservations strongly recommended. Deliveries on orders over $40. Takeouts. MC, VI, AE, DC, CB. Out-of-town checks OK with ID.

Hong Kong Cafe
Chinese
2 S. Mills St., Madison / 608-259-1668
(At the corner of Mills & Regent Sts., near the hospital/medical complex)

Here is a popular Chinese restaurant in the campus area, and one of the few to serve dim sum, on weekends. (Dim sum, for the uninitiated, is the serving of many different appetizers or small dishes. It is a delightful custom, and one way to sample the restaurant's cuisine in a relaxed manner.) The regular menu carries a wide array of traditional Chinese-American dishes, from moo shu pork to fra-grant beef and cashew chicken, to Hong Kong duck and double color shrimp. For dependable Chinese food in the campus area, I can recommend this little family cafe.

Inexpensive. Most dinners $5-10. Serving Sun.-Thurs. 11-9:30, Fri.-Sat. 11-10:30. Curb parking. Wheelchair accessible. Smoking & nonsmoking sections. Full bar. Reservations recommended. Local deliveries. Takeouts. Catering service. MC, VI, Dis. Out-of-town checks OK with ID.

Husnu's
Italian / Turkish
547 State St., Madison / 608-256-0900
(Near the campus end of State St.)

Husnu's was one of the first truly exotic restaurants to arrive in Madison, in 1978, and it has been very successful ever since with a combination of Turkish and Italian cuisines. If the mixture sounds unusual, it's because the owner and chef, Husnu Atis, grew up in Turkey but also worked in Italian restaurants. Obviously, the two cuisines thrive very well together. Lamb shish kebab, followed by cappuccino torte or ricotta cheesecake, is something to write home about. The menu has increasingly been dominated by fresh seafood—salmon, scallops, shrimp, swordfish, and more—in keeping with today's demand for lighter and reduced fat dining. All are well prepared, some with spicy sauces. The appetizers and soups here are worth writing home about, as well. Stuffed grape leaves, artichokes stuffed with Parmesan cheese and chopped shrimp, hearty chicken soups, all are expertly prepared. All meals come with the traditional flat Middle Eastern bread, which is made right in the restaurant.

Inexpensive to moderate. Most dinners $7-13. Serving daily 9 am-11 pm. Sun brunch 10-2. Nearby parking ramp. Wheelchair accessible. Totally nonsmoking. Beer & wine served. Children's portions. Reservations recommended. Takeouts. MC, VI. Out-of-town checks OK with ID.

The Ivy Inn
American
2355 University Ave., Madison / 608-233-4375
(On the near-west side, on "old" University Ave.)

The Ivy Inn is a comfortable restaurant serving a wide selection of American foods. Many of its loyal customers are visitors to the nearby Veterans Hospital or the UW Hospitals and Clinics. The Ivy serves a popular vegetarian brunch on the first and third Sunday of each month, a vegetarian buffet every Saturday evening, and features heart-healthy menu items at all times. We also think it has one of the best Friday night fish fries around.

Inexpensive to moderate. Most dinners $7-12. Serving Mon.-Sat. 7-2 & 5-8, Fri. dinner until 9, Sun. breakfast buffet 7-10, brunch 10-2. Closed Sun. eve. Parking lot. Wheelchair accessible. Smoking & nonsmoking sections. Cocktail lounge. Reservations accepted for parties of 6 or more. Private parties (max. 95). MC, VI, AE, DC. Out-of-town checks OK with ID.

Kabul Restaurant
Afghani / Mediterranean
541 State St., Madison / 608-256-6322
(On popular State St., between the Capitol and the UW campus)

When you're feeling a little adventurous, Kabul welcomes you with exciting, well-prepared, and surprisingly moderate-priced specialties from Afghanistan and the Mediterranean region. Kabul was founded in 1990 by Ghafoor Zafari, one of two brothers who established the popular Second Story Restaurant (across the street) in 1979. Specialties at Kabul include grilled marinated kebobs, fresh fish, couscous, steamed scallion-filled dumplings, poultry dishes, and many vegetarian entrees. Kabul's Afghani flat bread is so popular that it is now distributed around town and is available for patrons to take home.

Inexpensive. Most dinners $7-10. Serving Sun.-Thurs. 11-10:30, Fri.-Sat. 11-11. Nearby public parking ramps. Dining area wheelchair accessible (but not rest rooms). Smoking & nonsmoking sections. Full bar. Reservations recommended. Takeouts. MC, VI, AE, DC, CB . Out-of-town checks OK with ID.

Kosta's
Greek / American
117 State St., Madison / 608-155-6671
(On upper State St., near the Capitol)

Kosta's specializes in Greek foods, but has enough American dishes on the menu to please even those who eschew culinary adventure. The atmosphere is relaxed and pleasant, yet maintains touches of elegance with white linen and candlelight. Specialties include a flaming cheese appetizer, Greek salads, gyros, and kebabs, but you'll also find chicken breast royale, Pacific stuffed salmon, and phyllo-wrapped chicken. A popular after-work meeting place for Capitol-area employees, Kosta's offers ten beers on tap and more than thirty wines by the glass.

Inexpensive to moderate. Most dinners $8-13.Serving Sun. 4-10, Mon.-Fri. 11-10, Sat. 4-11. Nearby public parking ramps. Wheelchair accessible. Smoking & nonsmoking sections. Cocktail lounge/bar. Children's portions. Reservations recommended. Takeouts. Catering service. Private parties (max. 75). MC, VI, AE, DC, CB.

Lao Laan-Xang
Laotian
6824 Odana Rd., Madison / 608-829-2405

Of all the Asian restaurants in Madison—and there were more than 40 at last count—Lao Laan-Xang is one of the most interesting, and certainly one of our favorites. The cuisine here is dominated by coconut milk, lemon grass, chili peppers, peanut sauce, and, of course, rice. The menu lists a broad array of soups, salads, noodle and fried-rice dishes, and entrees featuring seafood, duck, and vegetables. But Lao Laan-Xang is best known, and deservedly so, for its curry. One of our favorites is Kang Phet, made with beef, bamboo shoots, eggplant, chilies, and basil, served with a sauce made of chilies, shrimp paste, onion, garlic, and lemon grass. The restaurant is on Madison's far west side, near West Towne. It's set back in a strip mall, so you'll have to look for it.

Inexpensive. Most dinners $6-10. Serving Sun.-Thur. 11-9, Fri.-Sat. 11-10. Parking lot. Wheelchair accessible. Smoking & nonsmoking sections. Cocktail lounge. Children's menu. Reservations recommended. Takeouts. Catering service. Private parties (max. 35). MC, VI, AE. No checks.

★ ★ ★
L'Escargot
Continental / French
2784 S. Fish Hatchery Rd., Madison / 608-273-2666

Owner and chef Tomas Ballesta was trained at the prestigious Paris Cordon Bleu, and plied his skill in several countries before coming to the United States, where he opened L'Escargot in 1977. His culinary style is classic Continental, depending on fresh foods of high quality, excellent sauces, and classic recipes, using fresh fish, beef, veal, chicken, and rabbit. The restaurant, located south of the Beltline, is intimate and romantic, a place where you would want to celebrate an anniversary. There are several small dining rooms, and the service is attentive without being intrusive. L'Escargot, in other words, is a genuine class act. (Don't miss the escargot a la Bourguignonne.)

Expensive. Most dinners $17-23. Serving weekdays 6-10 pm, Fri.-Sat. 6-10:30. Closed Sun. Parking lot. Wheelchair accessible. Smoking & nonsmoking sections. Full bar. Some children's portions. Reservations recommended. Private parties (max. 55). MC, VI, AE, DC, CB.

★ ★ ★
L'Etoile

American / Midwest regional
25 N. Pinckney St., Madison / 608-251-0500
(On the Capitol Concourse)

L'Etoile is, by any criteria used, the best restaurant in Madison. Founded in 1976 by Odessa Piper and run by her since then, this upstairs restaurant—"The Star"—turns out some of the most creative, thoughtful, and well-prepared dishes of any restaurant in the Midwest. The decor is simple and elegant, with exposed brick walls, hanging green plants, and fresh flowers on every table. The emphasis is squarely on the food. Not content to imitate a French or Continental style, L'Etoile uses the best of Midwestern foods in creating imaginative, satisfying, and often exciting recipes. Ms. Piper can often be seen shopping for fresh organic produce at the Madison Farmer's Market, which is held on Saturdays and Wednesdays during the season. The menu at L'Etoile changes frequently—indeed, it is printed anew every afternoon, taking advantage of the fresh foods that have arrived that morning. The results are always rewarding, sometimes spectacular. Here are some items from just one day's summer menu: dill, chive, and tarragon pestos set in new potatoes with soured cream. Fresh goat cheese and green garlic appetizer baked in a squash blossom. Crawfish, pork sausage, roasted peppers and grilled sweetcorn in a spicey crawfish broth. Tenderloin of American Bison with Kingsfield Garden's Beefsteak tomatoes, summer herb vinaigrette and fried haystack potatoes. Brambleberry crepes with wild blackberry ice cream. Get the idea? For any truly special occasion, you could not plan a more memorable meal than one at L'Etoile.

Expensive. Most dinners $18-25. Serving Mon.-Fri. 5:30 to closing, Sat. 5 to closing. Closed Sun. Nearby parking ramps. Not wheelchair accessible. Totally nonsmoking. Cocktail lounge/bar. Small children not encouraged. Reservations recommended. MC, VI, DC. Out-of-town checks OK with ID.

Leske's

Supper Club
6401 Monona Dr., Monona / 608-222-8646
(1/4 mi N from Hwys. 12/18 at Monona Dr. exit)

Leske's, established in 1958, is virtually the last of the old-time, traditional supper clubs left in Madison, a city that has been captured by low-fat, ethnic, and trendy culinary styles of the '90s. While once the city's restaurants were dominated by supper clubs, now Leske's stands at the city gates, virtually alone. Here, the menu still features shrimp cocktail, broasted chicken baskets, steaks and chops, "steak 'n tail," smoked barbequed ribs, lobster tail, and french-fried just about everything. And those who love this traditional fare still flock to Leske's, especially on Friday night for the fish fry—boiled cod or fried perch with fried potatoes, coleslaw, relishes, rolls and butter. There are specials every night at Leske's, including steamed shrimp, pork loin and dressing, fried catfish, chicken and dumplings, and—on Saturday night—prime rib. For traditional supper club dining in the Capitol City, Leske's is your choice.

Inexpensive to moderate. Most dinners $6-12. Serving Sun. breakfast 10-1, dinner 11-11, Mon.-Sat. 11-11. Parking lot. Dining area wheelchair accessible (but not rest rooms). Smoking & nonsmoking sections. Cocktail lounge/bar. Children's menu. Reservations recommended. Takeouts. Catering service. Live classic rock and country music Wed. thru Sat. nights. Private parties (max. 50). MC, VI. Out-of-town checks OK with ID.

Lombardino's
Italian
2500 University Ave., Madison / 608-238-1922

This cheerful Italian garden restaurant is one of Madison's oldest, serving Sicilian specialties since 1943. It is located on "old" University Avenue (that part cut off by Campus Drive), across from the InnTowner hotel and close to the Veterans and University of Wisconsin hospitals. The atmosphere is casual and relaxed, with Italian antiques and artifacts—including a ceramic miniature reproduction of the Fountain of Trevi—sprinkled throughout the restaurant.

Inexpensive to moderate. Most dinners $6-15. Serving dinner Sun. 4-9, weekdays 4:30-10, Fri.-Sat. 4:30-11. Parking lot. Wheelchair accessible. Smoking & nonsmoking sections. Cocktail lounge. Families encouraged. Children's menu. Children's birthday parties arranged. "Early bird" special prices for seniors (62). Private parties catered Mon. night only. MC, VI, Dis. Out-of-town checks OK with ID.

Lu Lu's
Arabic / Middle Eastern
2524 University Ave., Madison / 608-233-2172

This charming and popular spot on "old" University Avenue is Madison's favorite Middle Eastern restaurant, owned and operated by a friendly Palestinian family. Specialties include shish kebab, lamb dishes, baba ghanoug, lentil soup, couscous, falafel, and variations on tabuli and hummus. There are also many vegetarian dishes and wonderful salads. A special feature is the "Dewan," which is a secluded pillow room, perfect for romantic dinners in the Sultan's manner. (Be sure to reserve the Dewan in advance.)

Moderate. Most dinners $7-10. Open 11-9 weekdays, 11-9:30 Fri. & Sat. Closed Sun. Curbside parking. Wheelchair accessible. Beer & wine. Takeouts. Totally nonsmoking. MC, VI. Out-of-town checks OK with ID.

The Mandarin Palace Crab House
Chinese / Seafood
6722 Odana Rd., Madison / 608-833-8498

Located on Madison's far-west side, this is an excellent Chinese restaurant that specializes in fresh shellfish and other seafood. Appetizers include steamed mussels, oysters on the halfshell, and fried calamari. Entrees feature live Maine lobster, Dungeness crab, New Orleans soft-shell crab, ocean scallops, sauteed ginger oyster, braised bass with bean sauce, governor's shrimp, and more. There are also pork, chicken, duck, beef, lamb, and vegetarian dishes. Highlights are the daily lunch buffet, at $4.99, and Mongolian barbeque, cooked at tableside.

Moderate. Most dinners $8-13. Serving Mon.-Thurs. 11:30-2 & 4-10, Fri.-Sat. 11:30-11, Sun. 12-9 (brunch 12-2:30). Parking lot. Wheelchair accessible. Smoking & nonsmoking sections. Cocktail lounge. Children's menu. Vegetarian entrees. Reservations recommended. Local deliveries & takeouts. Catering service. Private parties (max. 120). MC, VI, AE, Dis, DC. Out-of-town checks OK with ID.

The Mariner's Inn
Steakhouse / Seafood
5339 Lighthouse Bay Dr., Madison / 608-244-8418
(On the N shore of Lake Mendota, 1 blk W of junction of Hwy. 113
& Cty. Hwy. M. Turn on Westport Rd., cross bridge, go 1 blk
& turn R at the lighthouse.)

The Mariner's Inn is a beloved Madison institution run by the well-known Von Rutenberg family. This restaurant has had only two owners in 57 years, and it was a food-and-bar operation long before that. The Mariner's offers a romantic setting on the water, reachable by automobile, boat, or seaplane. The decor is nautical, with many fascinating marine artifacts scattered about, some antique. It is a favorite place to celebrate special occasions, or simply to enjoy great steaks, seafood (including shrimp, lobster, red snapper, and catch of the day), homemade hash browns, and Wisconsin cheesecake topped with Door County cherries.

Moderate to expensive. Most dinners $9-24. Serving daily from 4:30. Parking lot. Dining area wheelchair accessible (but not rest rooms). Smoking & nonsmoking sections. Cocktail lounge/bar. Children's birthday parties. Children's portions. Special "early bird" prices for seniors. Reservations recommended. Takeouts. Catering service. Private parties (max. 22). MC, VI. No checks.

Marrakesh Cafe
Moroccan
121 W. Main St., Madison / 608-255-1345
(Just off the Capitol Square, across from Inn on the Park)

This is the only Moroccan restaurant in town, as exotic a dining experience as you will have in Wisconsin. There is a rich food tradition in Morocco, a prime agricultural region producing many fruits and vegetables for export to Europe. It is also a prime area for making wine and growing almonds and wheat. (Much of the wheat goes into the making of couscous, the base of many delectable North African dishes.) Morocco has also had long and frequent contact with both France and Spain, which has enhanced its culinary tradition. It all adds up to some fine dining at this excellent restaurant. Couscous is a staple, of course, with steamed vegetables, chicken, or lamb. There are other lamb dishes, some with sweet sauces, some spicy, all highly recommended. Favorite dishes here include Tajeen bel-berkook, which is lamb in a sauce of prunes and almonds. A house specialty is Tajeen bel-ghanmy—lamb stew with the diner's choice of vegetables—artichoke hearts, sweet peas, potatoes, olives, carrots, okra, and even anise. First-time visitors often go for the Couscous Royale, a signature dish at the Marrakesh, combing heaps of couscous with beef, lamb, or chicken, surrounded by an assortment of vegetables. Home-baked flat bread is served with each meal, as well as little side dishes of spiced vegetables. Also, don't miss the sensational mint tea, which is made with fresh mint leaves. If you are looking for a truly unique dining experience, the Marrakesh is definitely for you.

Inexpensive to moderate. Most dinners $8-14. Serving lunch Mon.-Fri. 11-2. Serving dinner Sun.-Thurs. 5-8:30, Fri. & Sat. 5-10. Nearby public parking ramp. Wheelchair accessible. Totally nonsmoking. Cocktail lounge/bar. Children's birthday parties. Reservations recommended on weekends. Local deliveries. Take-outs. MC, VI. Out-of-town checks OK with ID.

Monty's Blue Plate
American classic diner
2089 Atwood Ave., Madison / 608-244-8505
(On the near-east side, across from the Barrymore Theatre)

Here is one of the most popular dining spots on the east side, an old gas station restored and turned into a classic American diner. Cool blue neon accents lots of chrome and stainless steel, and music from the 1940s plays in the background—Sinatra, Goodman, Armstrong, Fitzgerald. And the food is better than nearly any classic diner you've ever visited. Monty's has taken ordinary diner food—hamburgers, meat loaf, chicken—and elevated every dish into something extra-special. There is also fresh fish, pasta, exotic vegetarian dishes, and unique sandwiches. The spicy waffle fries are a specialty of the house, and the daily soups are outstanding. At these bargain prices, you can't go wrong at the Blue Plate. Plus, the service is friendly and efficient.

Inexpensive. Most dinners $7-10. Serving Sun.-Thurs. 7:30 am-9 pm (to 10 pm in summer), Fri. 7 am-10 pm (to 11 pm in summer), Sat. 7:30 am-10 pm (to 11 pm in summer). Parking lot. Wheelchair accessible. Totally nonsmoking. Beer & wine served. Children's menu. Vegetarian entrees. Reservations not accepted. Takeouts. Catering service. MC, VI. Out-of-town checks OK with ID.

The New Seoul
Korean
2503 University Ave., Madison / 608-238-3331
(On "old" University Ave., across from Lombardino's)

This small, family-run restaurant specializes in Korean foods such as Bul go gi—char-broiled beef ribs, beef, chicken, and pork. There are also authentic Korean stir-fries, and some soups hot and spicy enough to warm the cockles of your heart—and perhaps blow off the top of your head—on a cold Wisconsin winter's evening. The Lee family is proud that none of the recipes are Americanized in any way, but are the same as those served in Korea. With a bottle or two of cold Korean beer, a dinner at the New Seoul can be a truly heartwarming experience.

Inexpensive to moderate. Most dinners $6-13. Serving Mon.-Sat. lunch 11-2:30, dinner 4-9. Closed Sun. Parking lot in back of restaurant. Dining area wheelchair accessible (but only women's rest room is wheelchair accessible). Smoking & nonsmoking sections. Beer served. Reservations recommended. Takeouts. MC, VI. No checks.

Otto's Restaurant & Bar
American / Continental
6405 Mineral Point Rd., Madison / 608-274-4044
(Just E of West Towne shopping mall, next to Oakwood Village)

Otto's is located in a charming 1879 stone farmhouse on Madison's far-west side. Using all three floors of the house (the bar is located downstairs) the restaurant imparts a feeling of elegant country intimacy. There is also an outdoor terrace for casual summer dining, and live jazz is played there on Wednesday nights during summer. Steaks are the specialty here, all of them certified black Angus beef. Comfort food is also emphasized. (Few upscale restaurants, for example, dare to include tuna-cheese casserole on the lunch menu!) Signature dishes include blackened T-bone with pecan butter, Chicken Pesto, Nate's Back Alley Ribs, and Pike Pistachio.

Moderate to Expensive. Most dinners $9-18. Serving weekdays 11:30-2:30 & 5:30-9:30, Fri. dinner until 10. Sat. dinner only, 5:30-10. Closed Sun. Parking lot. Wheelchair accessible. Cocktail lounge. Reservations recommended. Takeouts. Smoking & nonsmoking floors. Private parties (max. 35). MC, VI, AE, DC, CB. Out-of-town checks OK with ID.

Ovens of Brittany
Continental / Cafe / Bakery
305 State St., Madison / 608-257-7000
(On State St., between the Capitol and the UW campus)

The Ovens of Brittany, founded in 1971, was the first restaurant to bring true Continental and French-style cooking to Madison. The Ovens now operates four restaurants in Madison, in addition to a cafeteria in a bank building. It also operates the restaurant in the historic Chesterfield Inn, a bed-and-breakfast in Mineral Point, Wisconsin. Here at the original location, on State Street, the downstairs restaurant continues to serve in the Continental style, while the upstairs is more of a casual cafe and bakery. Specialties include chicken pot pie, quiche, stir-fries, fresh fish dishes, and omelets. The Ovens bakery has always been a Madison favorite, and the morning buns and croissants are still unbeatable in the area. Some of the more popular menu items are available in each of the Ovens' locations, while the manager or chef of each restaurant influences the remaining items. There is thus a connecting theme among all the restaurants, while each is allowed to express its individuality.

Moderate to expensive. Most dinners $10-19. Serving Sun. 9-9, Mon.-Thurs. 8-10, Fri.-Sat. 8-11. Nearby public parking ramps. Dining area wheelchair accessible (but rest rooms not wheelchair accessible). Totally nonsmoking. Cocktail lounge/bar. Children's menu. Vegetarian entrees. Seniors discount Mon. only (age 65+). Reservations recommended. Takeouts. Catering service. Private parties (max. 50). MC, VI, AE. Out-of-town checks OK with ID.

Ovens of Brittany
International / Bakery
1718 Fordem Ave., Madison / 608-241-7779
(From E. Johnson St., N on Fordem; restaurant immediately on left)

The east-side Ovens gained a solid reputation after the arrival of executive chef Howard Bender, and now ranks among the best restaurants in the area. Specialties include Yankee pot roast, spinach gateau, many vegetarian specialties, and fish and pasta dishes. There is a Sunday omelet bar, wonderful homemade soups, and homemade ice cream. This restaurant was established in 1984, in a strip mall, but a clever interior decorating scheme has turned it into a little piece of Victoriana.

Moderate to expensive. Most dinners $10-18. Serving Sun. 8 am-9 pm, Mon.-Thurs. 7 am-9 pm, Fri.-Sat. 7 am-9 pm. Parking lot. Wheelchair accessible. Smoking & nonsmoking sections. Cocktail lounge/bar. Children's menu. Vegetarian specialties. Seniors discount Mon. only (age 65+). Reservations recommended. Takeouts. Catering service. Fri. evening harp music. Private parties (max. 40). MC, VI, AE. Out-of-town checks OK with ID.

Ovens of Brittany
International / Bakery
3244 University Ave., Madison / 608-233-7701
(On the near-west side, in the Shorewood Shopping Center)

The Shorewood Ovens is architecturally striking. Designed by Herb De Levie, a student of Frank Lloyd Wright, it is built on several levels, providing visual interest and a sense of intimacy for diners (and added exercise for the servers). De Levie incorporated lots of wood into his design, made good use of a skylight, and even included a soothing waterfall and rock corner. When you're inside, it's hard to believe that this restaurant is in a strip mall. The menu here is typical Ovens, with chicken pot pie, sandwich melts, pasta dishes, and fresh fish dominating. There is an adjoining award-winning bakery (baked goods for the other Ovens restaurants come from here) with a takeout case for hungry office workers in a hurry.

Moderate to expensive. Most dinners $10-16. Serving Sun. 8 am-9 pm, Mon.-Thurs. 7 am-9 pm, Fri.-Sat. 7 am-10 pm. Parking lot. Wheelchair accessible. Smoking & nonsmoking sections. Cocktail lounge/bar. Children's menu. Vegetarian entrees. Seniors discount Mon. only (age 65+). Reservations accepted. Takeouts. Catering service. Live music some Sat. nights. Private parties (max. 40). MC, VI, AE. Out-of-town checks OK with ID.

Ovens of Brittany
Cafe / Bakery
1831 Monroe St., Madison / 608-251-2119
(Near Camp Randall stadium)

This is an Ovens in a small space, which has made it virtually into a neighborhood cafe—albeit one with that definite Ovens touch. The menu, again, is typically Ovens, with chicken pot pie, homemade soups, good, fresh salads, quiche, and lots of vegetarian entrees. Many west-side people who work downtown stop off here in the morning to pick up pastries for the office. Weekend shoppers on Monroe Street often meet here for brunch. Because of the limited space, there is often a wait for a table at this location, but it's one of the best restaurants in the area.

Moderate. Most dinners $8-13. Serving Sun. 8-8, Mon.-Sat. 7-9. Curb parking. Wheelchair accessible. Totally nonsmoking. Beer & wine served. Children's menu. Vegetarian entrees. Seniors discount Mon. only (age 65+). Takeouts. Catering service. MC, VI, AE. Out-of-town checks OK with ID.

Pasqual's
Southwestern American
2534 Monroe St., Madison / 608-238-4419
2098 Atwood Ave., Madison / 608-244-3142

With one restaurant on the near-east side and one on the near-west, Pasqual's has bracketed the central city with excellent Southwestern American cuisine. Both are sit-down restaurants, but takeouts are enormously popular, as weary central city workers stop by after work for tacos, burritos, and other take-home meals. Much of the culinary inspiration comes from northern New Mexico, the Santa Fe/Taos area—enchiladas with blue corn tortillas and green chili sauce, meal-size burritos, double tacos, and posole. There are cold Mexican bottled beers to wash it all down, and blue corn bread for dessert. For generous portions of good food at moderate prices, Pasqual's—on either side of town—is a decided hit.

Inexpensive. Most dinners under $6. Serving daily 10-10. Sat.-Sun. breakfast 8-12. Parking lot. Wheelchair accessible. Totally nonsmoking. Beer, wine, & margaritas are served. Reservations not accepted. Takeouts (call ahead for quick service). Catering service. MC, VI, AE. Out-of-town checks OK with ID.

Pasta per Tutti
Classic Italian
2009 Atwood Ave., Madison / 608-242-1800
(On the near-east side, at Schenk's Corners—corner of
Winnebago, Williamson, & Atwood)

Monty Schiro (of nearby Monty's Blue Plate) and chef Joe Sandretti opened this classic pasta house in the spring of 1993. The menu features three antipasti, two salads, an Italian vegetable soup with pesto and pasta, nine pasta dishes, and, for non-pasta lovers, beef tenderloin with shiitakes and garlic, and lamb chops with rosemary. The pasta here is the best in town. Some specialties include fettucine with artichokes and mushrooms, baked rigatoni in a white sauce with tomatoes and fontinella cheese, a seafood dish (shrimp, calamari, scallops, and mussels) with a garlic and white wine sauce over angel hair pasta, and linguine with chicken. There are good antipasti, two salads, and a nice Italian vegetable soup with garlic, pesto, and pasta. The decor here is subdued, with exposed brick walls, track lighting, and white linen tablecloths.

Moderate. Most dinners $8-15. Serving Sun.-Fri. 5:30-10, Sat. 5:30-11. Parking lot. Wheelchair accessible. Totally nonsmoking. Beer & wine served. MC, VI. Out-of-town checks OK with ID.

Peppino's
Italian
5518 University Ave., Madison / 608-233-2200

Peppino's has been serving classical Italian cuisine on University Avenue since 1974. This attractive restaurant features a romantic, candlelit atmosphere and dishes from several of Italy's regions. Specialties include veal Florentine, shrimp Livornese, whitefish piccante, and cassata Siciliana.

Moderate to expensive. Most dinners $10-18. Serving dinner Sun.-Thurs. 5-9:30, Fri.-Sat. 5-10:30. Parking lot. Wheelchair accessible. Smoking & nonsmoking sections. Cocktail lounge. Children are accommodated. Reservations recommended on weekends. Takeouts. Catering service. Private parties (max. 70). MC, VI, AE, DC, CB. Out-of-town checks OK with ID.

Pizzeria Uno
Italian
222 W. Gorham St., Madison / 608-255-7722
(Corner of Gorham & State St., near the University of Wisconsin campus and Capitol building)

This is one of the many restaurants that sprang from the famous "original" Pizzeria Uno, in Chicago. In Madison, it is a favorite among downtown business people, tourists, and UW college students. The bar is cool, urbane, beautiful, and lots of fun, and the service staff is one of the friendliest in town. Pizza, naturally, is the star attraction at Uno, and a mighty fine pizza it is—routinely voted best in Madison by several local reader polls. It is Chicago-style deep-dish pizza, the kind created more than a half-century ago by Chicago's Ike Sewell. There are also other Italian dishes, and very good salads. For lots of good food at quite modest prices, Pizzeria Uno is a good place to go in Madison.

Inexpensive. Most dinners $6-9. Serving daily from 11 am to bar closing. Public parking lot next door. Wheelchair accessible. 85% nonsmoking. Cocktail lounge/bar. Children's menu. Children's birthday parties. Reservations not accepted. Local deliveries. Takeouts. Catering service. MC, VI, AE, Dis. Out-of-town checks OK with ID.

Pizzeria Uno
Italian
7601 Mineral Point Rd., Madison / 608-833-7200
(On Mineral Point Rd., just W of West Towne shopping mall)

This is the "other" Pizzeria Uno in Madison, this one located on the far-west side of town in a historic 125-year-old stone farmhouse that has been uniquely restored. The menu is much the same as the downtown Uno's (see above). There is a beautiful outdoor patio for warm-weather dining from May through September.

Inexpensive. Most dinners $6-9. Serving daily from 11 am to bar closing. Parking lot. Wheelchair accessible. 90% nonsmoking. Cocktail lounge/bar. Children's menu. Children's birthday parties. Reservations not accepted. Local deliveries. Takeouts. Catering service. MC, VI, AE, Dis. Out-of-town checks OK with ID.

Porta Bella
Italian
425 N. Frances St., Madison / 608-256-3186
(Just 1 blk off State St., in the UW campus area)

This is one of the most romantic dining spots in the University of Wisconsin campus area. Elegant yet casual, its secluded corners, soft lighting, and a good wine list make it a popular spot for a special date or tete-a-tete. The basement wine bar is a popular spot for after work or after class socializing. House specialties include stuffed shrimp, chicken tetrazzini, ravioli, spedini, and the locally famous Porta salad.

Moderate. Most dinners $7-15. Open Sun-Thurs. 4:30-10:30, Fri. 11 am-midnight, Sat. 4:30-midnight. Nearby ramp parking. Wheelchair accessible. Cocktail lounge. Vegetarian entrees. Reservations recommended. Smoking & nonsmoking sections. Private parties (max. 38). MC, VI. Out-of-town checks OK with ID.

★ ★ ★
Quivey's Grove
Midwestern regional
6261 Nesbitt Rd., Madison / 608-273-4900
(Exit onto Nesbitt Rd. from Verona Rd., 2 mi S of Hwys. 12/18)

Quivey's Grove is located in a renovated 1855 stone house and stable listed on the National Register of Historic Buildings. There are five separate dining areas in the elegant Stone House, three in the Stable Tap & Grill, which is more casual and less expensive and separated from the Stone House by a tunnel. Of all the restaurants in the Madison area, Quivey's Grove is most attentive to regional heritage cooking, resulting in some unusual and quite delightful dishes. Rouladen Barstow, for instance, is a traditional German rolled beef stuffed with vegetables, sausage, bacon, and pickle. Pork Dewey (many dishes are named after local historic figures) is smoked pork loin served with sauerkraut and purees of sweet and white potatoes. Chicken Bond is a boneless breast with smoked duck stuffing and gorgonzola sauce, wild rice, and fresh vegetables, named after Wisconsin's own Carrie Bond, composer of "When you Come to the End of a Perfect Day" and other hits. Entrees in the Stable Tap & Grill are less ambitious albeit no less inviting—Verona Veal, Paoli Beef, Stew Waterloo, Daleyville Duck, and other dishes named after local communities. The desserts are memorable, as well, including chocolate steamed pudding, steamed gingerbread pudding, and apple crisp served warm and topped with vanilla ice cream. All the recipes are authentic, and all are made from scratch using real sweet butter, fresh cream, fresh potatoes, and the best and freshest of other ingredients. Quivey's Grove is simply one of the best restaurants in Wisconsin. Or, as the menu proclaims, "Quivey's Grove *is* Wisconsin."

Stone House: Moderate. Most dinners $13-16. Serving Sun. 5-9, Mon.-Thurs. 5:30-9, Fri.-Sat. 5-9:30. Reservations recommended.

Stable: Inexpensive to moderate. Most dinners $7-13. Serving Sun. 11-9, Mon.-Thurs. 11-10, Fri.-Sat. 11-11. Parking lot. Wheelchair accessible. Stone House is totally nonsmoking. Smoking permitted in bar only. Families with small children are encouraged to dine in the Stable Tap & Grill. Children's menu. Live piano music Fri. & Sat. nights. Private parties (max. indoors 40; outdoor tent holds 300 for private parties). MC, VI. Out-of-town checks OK with ID.

Saigon Restaurant
Vietnamese
6802 Odana Rd., Madison / 608-829-3727
(1 blk E of West Towne shopping mall)

The Saigon is a favorite of many Madisonians who appreciate regional Asian cuisine that is different from the standard Chinese-American fare. Saigon fills the bill quite nicely. Some of the Vietnamese specialties here include North Vietnamese rural soup, beef in 7 courses, lemon fish, chicken lemon grass, delicious Vietnamese chow mein, crab-and-asparagus soup, pork slices and pork balls en brochette, and barbequed pork kebabs. The egg rolls and spring rolls here are slender, wrapped in crisp rice-paper skins to cook quickly. This is certainly one of the best Oriental restaurants in Madison, and is highly recommended.

Inexpensive to moderate. Most dinners $6-15. Serving Sun.-Mon. 4:30-10, Tues.-Thurs. lunch 11-2:30, dinner 4:30-10. Fri.-Sat. lunch 11-2:30, dinner 4:30-11. Parking lot. Wheelchair accessible. Smoking & nonsmoking sections. Cocktail lounge/bar. Children's portions. Reservations recommended. Takeouts. Catering service. MC, VI. Out-of-town checks OK with ID.

The Second Story
Continental / Regional
508 State St., Madison / 608-256-2434
(In the heart of the University of Wisconsin campus area)

Since its inception in 1979, the Second Story has built a loyal clientele with its many intimate dining spaces overlooking Madison's State Street, the bustling artery that links the Capitol to the university campus. The Second Story offers fresh, creative salads and continental entrees, the most famous of which is Duck Strudel, a blend of lean duck, wild rice, and shiitake mushrooms, all wrapped in phyllo pastry, baked, and served with a carmelized cranberry-shallot wine sauce. The restaurant is also known for its nightly fresh fish specials and innovative sauces. The decor is art deco, primarily black and white, with many green plants. In the campus area, the Second Story is a good choice for outstanding Continental dining at most reasonable prices.

Moderate. Most dinners $8-15. Serving Sun. 5-9, Mon.-Sat. 11:30-2 & 5-9:30. Nearby public parking lots. Not wheelchair accessible. Smoking & nonsmoking sections. Cocktail lounge/bar. Children's portions. Reservations recommended. Takeouts. Live music on weekends. Private parties (max. 150). All major credit cards. Out-of-town checks OK with ID.

★ ★ ★

Smoky's Club
Steakhouse
3005 University Ave., Madison / 608-233-2120
(On the near-west side)

Local folks have long known that Smoky's has the best steaks in town, but now everybody knows. That happened when *Midwest Living* magazine ranked Smoky's as the best steakhouse in the Midwest. Since then, it has won top honors from the Knife and Fork Club of America, has been listed by *Northwest Airlines* magazine, and has received other widespread attention. The club is unassuming from the outside, but contains several sizeable dining rooms, all of which seem to be full of happy customers at all times. The menu here is traditional old-time supper club, with relish trays brought to every table, homemade soups, and side orders of cottage cheese, homemade hash browns (highly recommended), and pickled beets. There is chicken, and Canadian walleyed pike, and shrimp, but the main attraction, without doubt, is the steaks. Filet mignon, T-bone, New York strip, sirloin, ribeye, ground sirloin. Large or small, Smoky's steaks are simply the best—tender, well aged, never frozen, and perfectly cooked to order, with no tenderizer, no marinate. Steak just doesn't get any better than this.

Moderate to expensive. Most dinners $13-17. Serving 5-10 Mon. & Wed.-Sat. Closed Sun. & Tues. Parking lot. Wheelchair accessible. Smoking & nonsmoking sections. Cocktail lounge/bar. Limited reservations (but not accepted on Sat.). No credit cards. Out-of-town checks OK with ID.

Sunporch Cafe-Restaurant-Bakery
Contemporary American
2701 University Ave., Madison / 608-231-1111
(On the near-west side, 1 blk from UW & Veterans hospitals,
in Lakepoint Commons)

This bright and cheerful cafe specializes in contemporary American dishes with an ethnic flare. The menu changes with the seasons, taking advantage of the fresh foods available throughout the year. There are many vegetarian and heart-healthy dishes, wonderful breads and desserts made right in the cafe. Sunporch is a favorite place for friends and local business people to meet for breakfast or brunch, and of course it's a favorite weekend meeting place, as well. The atmosphere is relaxed, friendly, and comfortable. Sunporch is also an art gallery, with shows changing every six weeks.

Inexpensive to moderate. Most dinners $8-11. Serving Sun. 8 am-10 pm (brunch 8-3), Mon.-Thurs. 7 am-10 pm, Fri.-Sat. 7 am-11 pm. Parking lot. Wheelchair accessible. Totally nonsmoking. Full bar. Many vegetarian specialties. Children's portions on request. Reservations not accepted. Takeouts. Live jazz, classical, blues, & folk music Sun. eve. 6-9. MC, VI. Out-of-town checks OK with ID.

Sunprint Cafe & Gallery
Multi-ethnic
638 State St., Madison / 608-255-1555

Sunprint is a Madison institution. This campus-area cafe has been voted by the readers of several local newspapers as Madison's favorite lunch spot, and now it's making headlines in the dinner trade, too. Sunprint overlooks State Street, the busy and fascinating mall street that links the State Capitol to the University of Wisconsin campus. If you're lucky, you'll get a table by a window for great people-watching. Art exhibits change every six weeks, and all the art is for sale. The food speaks of several ethnic roots, including Italy and the Mediterranean. There are many vegetarian entrees, and the baked goods are outstanding. For value received, this is one of the best restaurants in Madison.

Inexpensive. Most dinners $6-11. Serving weekdays 7 am-10 pm, Fri.-Sat. until 11, Sun. 9-9 (brunch 9-5). Public parking ramps nearby. Not wheelchair accessible. Totally nonsmoking. Full bar. Children's portions. Vegetarian entrees. Reservations recommended for parties of 5 or more. Catering service. MC, VI. Out-of-town checks OK with ID.

Tanyeri Grill
Turkish
106 King St., Madison / 608-255-4700

Tanyeri is Madison's favorite Turkish restauant. In fact, it's Madison's *only* restaurant serving exclusively Turkish cuisine. Just a half-block off the Capitol Concourse, Tanyeri specializes in sauteed shrimp with feta cheese, kebabs, stuffed pita sandwiches, salads, baklava, and fruit vodka. This is a great place for vegetarians, with entree-size salads including grilled vegetable, tabuli, and feta-romaine, veggie sandwiches, and "Vegetarian Delight." The Eastern Anatolian yogurt soup is popular, as is the grilled salmon in grape leaves. Owner Kamil Tanyeri and chef Erol Andac are both natives of Istanbul, and have established a restaurant combining great food and a casual atmosphere.

Inexpensive. Most dinners $8-10. Serving weekdays 11-10, Fri.-Sat. 11-11. Closed Sun. Sidewalk cafe seating in summer. Public parking ramp nearby. Wheelchair accessible. Smoking & nonsmoking sections. Full bar. Children's portions on request. Vegetarian entrees. Reservations recommended on weekend nights. Takeouts. Catering service. Belly dancers one Saturday night each month. (Call.) MC, VI, AE. Local checks OK with ID.

The White Horse Inn / Appaloosa Room
Continental / Cajun / Southwestern
202 N. Henry St., Madison / 608-255-9933
(Just off State St. behind the Madison Civic Center)

This is a popular spot for Capitol-area workers to gather after a hard day at the office—the hors d'oeuvres are among the best in town—and they often decide to stay for dinner, as well. The White Horse features an extensive Continental menu. The salad bar here is outstanding, often voted "best in Madison" in several local reader polls. The Appaloosa Room, located above the White Horse, is a less formal restaurant, featuring a Cajun and Southwestern menu with tastes for all palates. Fresh fish, as well as many pasta dishes, are well represented in both restaurants.

White Horse: Moderate to expensive. Most dinners $14-18. **Appaloosa Room: Moderate.** Most dinners $9-16. Serving Sun. brunch 9-2, dinner 5-9. Mon.-Thurs. lunch 11-2:30, dinner 5-10. Fri. lunch 11-2:30, dinner 5-11. Sat. dinner 5-11. Nearby public parking ramp. Wheelchair accessible. Smoking & nonsmoking areas. Cocktail lounge/bar. Children's menu. Reservations recommended. Catering service. Private parties (max. 175). MC, VI, AE. No checks.

Wild Iris Cafe
Italian / Cajun / Cafe
1225 Regent St., Madison / 608-257-4747
(Near Camp Randall Stadium on the near-west side)

This is a popular lunch spot for people in the University of Wisconsin south campus area and for workers in the nearby hospital complex, and an equally popular dinner destination for people all over town who like imaginative dishes served at moderate prices. Specialties at this small cafe include owner/chef Anna Alberici's pasta dishes, and some spicy Cajun entrees.

Inexpensive. Most dinners under $10. Serving Sun. brunch 9-3, dinner 5-10. Lunch and dinner Mon.-Fri. 10:45-10. Sat. brunch 8-4, dinner 4-10. Curb parking. Dining area wheelchair accessible (but not rest rooms). Smoking & nonsmoking sections. Beer & wine served. Children's portions of some menu items. Takeouts. MC, VI. Out-of-town checks OK with management approval.

Wilson Street Grill
Contemporary American
217 S. Hamilton St., Madison / 608-251-3500
(Corner of Wilson & Hamilton Sts., 1-1/2 blks off Capitol Square)

The Wilson Street Grill is a bright, airy, and cheerful Capitol-area restaurant, much favored by many lawyers whose offices are in the area. There is an outdoor terrace for dining in warm weather, and the interior is decorated with fresh flowers and original art. The recipes are most inventive, using fresh, local foods whenever possible. On the menu, you'll find such specialties as Pizza Verona (with fresh spinach, red pepper, and eggplant), Southwestern black and red bean soup, Zuppa alla Marinara (Italian clam chowder), Panini Caponata (a sandwich with grilled eggplant, peppers, onions, goat cheese, and Calamata olives, served hot), grilled catfish with breadcrumb salsa, and a Wisconsin veal sausage plate (with three mustards). But the menu changes often, according to the season, and even steady patrons are often surprised and delighted at the innovations. There is a good selection of Wisconsin beers and American wines, and excellent designer coffees. Most of the entrees are light, making this a perennially popular lunch spot in the downtown area.

Moderate. Most dinners $7-11. Serving Mon.-Fri. 11-2 & 5:30-9:30. Sat. 5:30-10. Public parking ramps nearby. Free underground parking at restaurant after 4 pm. Wheelchair accessible. Smoking & nonsmoking sections. Cocktail lounge/bar. Reservations recommended (essential for Fri. dinner and for parties of 5 or more at lunch or dinner). Catering service. Private parties (max. 28). MC, VI. Out-of-town checks OK with ID.

Coachman's Inn
American
984 Cty. Hwy. A, Edgerton / 608-884-8484
(From I-90 & Hwy. 51, take Exit #156, Stoughton)

This restaurant, styled in the fashion of an English country inn, has been owned and operated by the Johnson family for more than thirty years. Roast duck, veal, and charcoal-grilled steaks are the specialties here. There are also stuffed shrimp, orange roughy in lobster sauce, chicken dishes (including chicken a la Coachman, stuffed with mushrooms, broccoli, and Swiss cheese). Prime rib is the special on Wednesday, Saturday, and Sunday nights. The salad bar is a high point of Coachman's Inn, everything made fresh in their kitchen. In addition to the restaurant, there is a motel and a 27-hole golf course, so you can exercise, eat a good meal, and get a good night's sleep, all without moving your car.

Moderate: Most dinners $10-15. Serving Sun. brunch 9-2, dinner noon-9, week-days 11-4 & 4:30-9, Fri.-Sat. 11-4 & 4:30-10. Parking lot. Dining area wheelchair accessible (but not rest rooms). Main dining room is nonsmoking. Smoking is allowed in cocktail lounge/bar. Children's portions. Reservations recommended. Takeouts. Private parties (max. 200). MC, VI, AE, Dis. Out-of-town checks OK with ID.

Homestead Restaurant
American
3223 Hwy. JG North, Mt. Horeb / 608-437-5439
(2 mi N of Mt. Horeb on Hwy. JG, through Stewart Park)

The Homestead is like a page out of *Country Living* magazine, from the maple dining furniture to the country curtains on the windows. The menu is attuned to country living, also, with pan-fried pork chops, Swiss steak, wild rice soup, and Schaum torte the specialties of the house. The setting for the Homestead is an idyllic pastoral scene, with green, rolling hills and flowers blooming everywhere (in season, that is). This is a favorite place for wedding rehearsal dinners and receptions, and for weddings themselves. It is also a favorite place to take Mother on her special day. There is a large gift shop filled with country-type things.

Inexpensive to moderate. Most dinners $7-14. Serving Sun. 11-7, Tues.-Sat. 11-8. Closed Mon. Parking lot. Wheelchair accessible (lower dining level only). Smoking & nonsmoking sections. Full bar. Children's portions. Reservations recommended. Private parties (max. 23). MC, VI. Out-of-town checks OK with ID.

★ ★ ★
Pronto Pizza / Sole e Sapori
An Italian Eatery
209 E. Main St., Mt. Horeb / 608-437-4987
(On Business Hwy. 18/151, in downtown Mt. Horeb)

Pronto Pizza is about as close to a true southern Italian *trattoria* as you will find in the Midwest—except that the food is better. One taste of the Vitale family's homemade pasta and sauce will tell you that you have found a diamond in the rough, for this unassuming little eatery has, in my opinion, the best Italian food in Wisconsin—in truth, the best I have had anywhere, including Italy. Chicken marsala. Veal scallopini. Fettuccine Alfredo. Tortellini. Spaghetti. Each more heavenly than the other. The antipasto includes real Italian olives, tomatoes, caviar. The garlic bread, topped with melted cheese, is worth writing home about (or leaving home for). The stuffed pizza is *classico*. And Sam Vitale's *tiramisu* is, beyond a doubt, a world-class dessert. Don't look for fancy trappings when you come to Pronto. But do look for simply superb Italian food, all at most modest prices.

Inexpensive. Most dinners under $8. Serving Sun.-Thurs. 4-10, Fri.-Sat. 4-10:30. Easy curb parking. Wheelchair accessible. Children's birthday parties. Children's portions. Beer & wine served. Reservations not accepted. Deliveries. Takeouts. Catering service. No policy on smoking. Private parties (max. 14). No credit cards. Out-of-town checks OK with ID.

Chalet Landhaus
Swiss
801 Hwy. 69, New Glarus
608-527-5234 or 1-800-944-1716
(On Hwy. 69, 25 mi S of Madison)

This Swiss-American restaurant, located inside the Chalet Landhaus Motel, is a popular one among tourists and locals alike. The menu is very, very Swiss, offering wiener schnitzel, piccata schnitzel, jager schnitzel, and several other schnitzels. There are fish spetzialitaten, including baby perch, fresh salmon, and Dover sole, and other chalet spetzialitaten, including beef fondue, gourmet fondue (beef, shrimp, scallops, and lobster chunks), and, of course, geschnetzeltes, which are tiny medallions of veal served with a wine and mushroom sauce. The Landhaus is proud of its traditional Swiss house salad, not found anywhere else in the area. For a complete meal, there are also fresh baked goods and desserts from the Landhaus' own bakery.

Moderate to expensive. Most dinners $11-17. Serving Sun. breakfast buffet 7-12. Dinner Tues.-Thurs. 5:30-9, Fri.-Sat. 5:30-10. No dinner served Sun. Closed Mon. Parking lot. Wheelchair accessible. Smoking & nonsmoking sections. Cocktail lounge/bar. Children's portions on request. Reservations recommended. Catering service. Private parties (max. 70). MC, VI, AE, Dis. Out-of-town checks OK with ID.

Glarner Stube
Swiss
518 First St., New Glarus / 608-527-2216

The Glarner Stube is located in a 1901 building in downtown New Glarus. Debbie Anderegg and Gary Westby took over the restaurant in 1991, and now serve a wide variety of outstanding Swiss specialties. The decor is relaxed and very Swiss, and there is a beautiful old bar. Some of the house specialties here are cheese fondue, wiener schnitzel, and Swiss sausages, but the restaurant is perhaps best known for its Swiss vegetable soup and roesti potatoes, made with Swiss cheese. The menu also lists Swiss meatballs, bratwurst, and geschnetzlets. There is a lunch menu featuring sandwiches and platters of chicken or fried shrimp, and a special section of the menu for light eaters.

Inexpensive to moderate. Most dinners $8-14. Serving Sun.-Thurs. 11-8, Fri.-Sat. 11-10. Closed Mon. in winter. Easy curb parking. Not wheelchair accessible. Staff tries to separate smokers and nonsmokers. Cocktail lounge/bar. Children's menu. Takeouts. Catering service. MC, VI. Out-of-town checks OK with ID.

New Glarus Hotel
Swiss-German
100 Sixth Ave., New Glarus / 608-527-5244
(In downtown New Glarus)

The New Glarus Hotel is the best known of the New Glarus Swiss restaurants. It was founded in 1853, and has been under present ownership since 1975. The atmosphere is strictly "old world," with Swiss-style woodwork and warm lighting. The outside of the chalet-style building is decorated with scores of flower boxes and baskets in summer, and there is a popular glassed-in dining balcony overlooking Main Street. This restaurant is renowned for its Swiss-German cuisine, and especially for its veal dishes, wiener schnitzel, cordon bleu, geschnetzlets, pork dishes, and its cheese and beef fondues. One of the highlights here is the spectacular Sunday brunch, featuring nearly two dozen Swiss specialties—delicate veal sausage, light cheese pies with ham, pork with sauerkraut, geschnetzlets, barbecued meatballs, baked ham, roast beef, heaps of homemade baked goods, and much more. One brunch here will make any further dining that day an exercise in redundancy.

Inexpensive to moderate. Most dinners $8-15. Serving Sun. 10:30-9, Mon.-Thurs. 11-9, Fri.-Sat. 11-10. Sun. brunch 10:30-3. Easy curb parking. Wheelchair accessible. Smoking & nonsmoking sections. Cocktail lounge/bar. Children's birthday parties. Children's menu. Reservations recommended. Takeouts. Catering service. Live polka and old-time music Fri. & Sat eves. Private parties (max. 200). MC, VI, AE, Dis.

The Prairie Inn
Supper club
Hwys. 22 & 60, off Hwy. 51, North Leeds, Arlington / 608-635-7272
(20 minutes N of Madison)

"Good, old-fashioned country dinners" says it all for the Prairie Inn. Hosts
Jim and Pam Childs, who have operated the restaurant for more than a decade,
have created a lovely atmosphere for relaxed dining. The club is decorated with
antiques, barnboard, stained glass, and a cozy fireplace. All the favorite Wisconsin supper club staples are on the menu—steaks, chicken, shrimp, and lobster
tails—and there are nightly specials, including deep-fried or baked cod and
prime rib on Saturday nights. A popular favorite is "Ton on a Tin," combining
cod, shrimp, ribs, and chicken with coleslaw, baked beans, potato, and corn on
the cob. For intimate dining, there are four private rooms.

Inexpensive: Most dinners $8-10. Serving dinner Tues., Wed., Thurs. & Sun. 5-9,
Fri. & Sat. 5-10. Bar open 3 pm. Parking lot. Dining rooms wheelchair accessible
(but not rest rooms). No policy on smoking. Cocktail lounge/bar. Children's
menu. Reservations recommended. Takeouts. No credit cards. Out-of-town checks
OK with ID.

★ ★ ★

Luther's
Continental / Regional
1648 Cty. Rd. N, Stoughton / 608-873-5600

Luther's prefers to keep a low profile in the Madison area, and as a result many
people have never even heard of it. Nevertheless, it is one of the finest restaurants
in Wisconsin, truly a hidden gem. It is, in fact, hidden in the basement of a former
orphanage, right in the middle of a private campground. How's that for hidden?
As you drive up to the entrance of this institutional-looking brick building, you
might think that you have come to the wrong place. but step through the front
door and into the basement, and another world awaits you. The intimate bar is
cozily decorated and stocked with richly upholstered club furniture. The dining
room is tasteful and subdued, the tables fitted with white linen and holding candles, sparkling glassware, white china, and fresh red carnations in bud vases. The
menu lists a dozen or so entrees—classic variations of beef, veal, trout, pheasant,
pork, and duckling. A favorite appetizer is a fresh round of rye bread, hollowed
out and filled with a dill dip containing crabmeat, pecans, walnuts, and almonds.
The wild mushroom soup is outstanding. A green salad features crisp romaine,
cucumbers, shiitake mushrooms, and a light raspberry vinaigrette. A small sorbet
is served before the entree. I once enjoyed medallions of beef with two sauces—
one a brandy-based reduction sauce, the other a pink peppercorn sauce based in

beef stock and cabernet sauvignon. The lamb chops with plum sauce are wonderful, as is the pork Wellington. Luther's desserts are equally memorable. I will always remember the pecan-walnut-caramel-bourbon pie. The sheer culinary artistry practiced at this unlikely restaurant makes it all the more treasured by its limited but loyal clientele. I was sorely tempted to withhold it from this book, for selfish reasons, but in the end could not do so.

Expensive. Most dinners $14-20. Serving Wed.-Sat. 6-9. Parking lot. Not wheelchair accessible. Smoking only in the lounge. Cocktail lounge/bar. Small children not encouraged. Reservations essential. Catering service. Private parties (max. 50). MC, VI, AE. Out-of-town checks OK with ID.

Old Swiss House
Swiss / American
Hwy. 51, Stoughton / 608-251-2800
(On Hwy. 51 between McFarland & Stoughton)

Here, in a part of Wisconsin dominated by Norwegian-American culture, Kurt and Heidi Ruefenacht have brought a refreshing touch of their native Switzerland. The atmosphere is cozy and relaxing. There is a fine view of Lake Kegonsa and there is outdoor dining on the deck in summer. In winter, cozy up to the fireplace in the bar. The menu features traditional Swiss items such as rahmschnitzel (veal with mushroom sauce), roesti (hash browns made with Swiss cheese), sausages, fondues, veal dishes, and fresh fish specialties. The Sunday champagne brunch is impressive, featuring more than thirty items, everything homemade in the Old Swiss House kitchen. For authentic Swiss cuisine in this part of the state, you couldn't do better.

Inexpensive to moderate. Most dinners $8-15. Serving dinner Sun. 2:30-9, Tue-Sat. 4:30-10. Sun. brunch 10-2. Closed Mon. Parking lot. Wheelchair accessible. Smoking & nonsmoking sections. Cocktail lounge/bar. Children's menu. Reservations recommended. Takeouts. Catering service. MC, VI, AE, Dis. Out-of-town checks OK with ID.

The O'Malley Farm Cafe
Cafe
403 W. Main St., Waunakee / 608-849-7401
(At the corner of Hwys. 9/113/19)

As Pat O'Malley says, the cafe is "only ten minutes north of Madison!" This sprawling and comfortable country cafe, decorated with farm antiques, is best known for its big breakfasts—especially Sunday brunch—but Pat is also proud of his Irish stew, ribs, fresh turkey buffet, and the popular Friday night fish fry. It's a great place to bring the family—and a big appetite. Try the hobo breakfast, for instance—hash browns covered with melted American cheese, topped with bacon and two eggs, and served with homemade biscuits, butter, and honey. There are specials nightly, including baked ham, oven-roasted turkey with all the trimmings, and spaghetti and meatballs. On Saturday there is roast pork loin,on Sunday there is baked chicken, and on Friday? Of course, a fish fry!

Inexpensive. Most dinners $6-8. Open Sat.-Thurs. 6 am-9 pm (8 pm in winter), Fri. until 10 pm. Sun. brunch 8-2. Parking lot. Seniors discount (age 62+). Wheelchair accessible. Children's birthday parties. Children's menu. Full bar. Reservations recommended. Takeouts. Private parties (max. 90). MC, VI. Out-of-town checks OK with ID.

MIDDLETON

Chalet St. Moritz
Swiss / French / American
4635 Chalet St., Middleton / 608-836-7151
(4 mi W of Hwy. 12 on Airport Rd.)

The Chalet St. Moritz is nestled in the lush, rolling Wisconsin countryside. It's chalet-style building and Swiss decor offer elegant and relaxed dining with an old-world touch. Specialties here include beef and cheese fondues, wiener schnitzel, roesti, spaetzle, veal dishes, steaks, prime rib, and Chateaubriand flambe. Patrons also like the flaming cherries jubilee and flaming peaches. (A lot of brandy here goes up in flames.) Wedding parties are a specialty of Chalet St. Moritz, and in fact a chapel is available for the event.

Moderate to expensive. Most dinners $9-19. Serving dinner Mon. & Wed.-Sat. 5-10. Closed Sun. & Tues. (except for private parties of 25 or more). Parking lot. Wheelchair accessible. Smoking & nonsmoking sections. Cocktail lounge/bar. Children's portions. Reservations essential. Takeouts Fri. only. Dancing & live accordion music and yodeling Fri. eves. Private parties (max. 280). MC, VI, AE. Out-of-town checks OK with ID.

The Gallery
Continental / French
1904 Parmenter St., Middleton / 608-831-5000
(1 blk S of University Ave. at the only 4-way stop in town)

The Gallery is housed in an 1850 building that was once the American House hotel. It was famous for its Sunday night 25¢ chicken dinners, which regularly attracted hundreds of University of Wisconsin students from nearby Madison. There are no more 25¢ chicken dinners, but there are still plenty of hearty dinners at moderate prices at the Gallery. The restaurant today is in a romantic garden setting, with a beautiful greenhouse dining room and lots of plants, ponds, and stone walls scattered throughout the restaurant. It's a popular place for weddings and receptions. The broad menu features a variety of seafood, poultry, pork, lamb, and beef dishes. Some specialties are poached whitefish, seafood en croute, chicken and shrimp marengo, and stuffed chicken breast florentine. The menu includes a selection of light entrees, and there are specials on Thursday, Friday, and Saturday nights. Tempting desserts include truffles, cheesecake, and choco-late mousse.

Moderate. Most dinners $11-14. Serving Sun. 10:30-2 (brunch), Mon.-Sat. lunch 11:30-2, Thurs.-Sat. dinner 5-10. Nearby public parking. Easy curb parking. Wheelchair accessible. Smoking & nonsmoking sections. Cocktail lounge/bar. Gift shop. Children's portions. Takeouts. Private parties (max. 140). MC, VI. Out-of-town checks OK with ID.

Imperial Garden
Chinese
2038 Allen Blvd., Middleton / 608-238-6445
(At the corner of University Ave. & Allen Blvd.)

The Imperial Garden, which also has a restaurant on Madison's east side, is annu-ally voted the Madison area's favorite Chinese restaurant. And small wonder, since it does everything so incredibly well, and does it in the most bright and cheerful of surroundings. It specializes in Mandarin and Szechuan cuisine, includ-ing cashew chicken, fragrant shrimp, Mongolian beef, and fresh seafood dishes. Other favorite dishes include mussels with black bean sauce, Governor's beef, and Singapore beef. But everything at the Imperial Garden is highly recommended. It's a Chinese restaurant where you just can't go wrong.

Inexpensive to moderate. Most dinners $8-13. Serving Sun. 11:30-9, Mon.-Thurs. 11:30-2 & 4-9:30, Fri. 11:30-2 & 4-10:30, Sat. 4-10:30. Parking lot. Wheelchair accessible. Separate smoking & nonsmoking dining rooms. Cocktail lounge/bar. Children's portions. Reservations recommended. Takeouts. Catering service. Private parties (max. 120). All major credit cards. Out-of-town checks OK with ID.

Sweeney's Stamm House
American supper club
6625 Century Ave., Middleton / 608-831-5835

The Stamm House is a Middleton landmark. Built in 1847, it is the oldest tavern in the county. The oak wood floor in the main dining room used to be a dance floor. Owner Jim Sweeney and family maintain the old-time flavor of the restaurant with red gingham curtains and knotty pine paneled walls. The Stamm House menu offers the hearty fare typical of Wisconsin supper clubs—homemade chicken and dumplings, barbecued pork ribs, corned beef and cabbage, and a Friday night all-you-can-eat fish fry. It's a casual spot, super-friendly, long popular with local families.

Inexpensive to moderate. Most dinners $7-13. Serving dinner Sun. 5-9, Tues.-Thurs. 5-9:30, Fri. 5-10, Sat. 5-9:30. Parking lot. Not wheelchair accessible. Smoking & nonsmoking sections. Cocktail lounge/bar. Takeouts. MC, VI. Local checks OK with ID.

Tiffany Grille
Holiday Inn Madison West
American / Regional
1313 John O. Hammons Dr., Middleton / 608-831-2000, ext. 7
(W from Hwy. 12 at Exit #252)

The Tiffany Grille is one of the most elegant dining spots in the area. It is located in the ten-story atrium of a big hotel and convention center, the Holiday Inn Madison West (which is actually located in east Middleton) and features a 55-foot waterfall and large potted tropical plants and trees. The menu gives several salutes to Wisconsin agricultural products with dishes such as deep-fried cheese curds, Wisconsin cheddar cheese and beer soup, and brook trout. There is also a full selection of fresh fish, steaks, poultry, and pork dishes. The restaurant is big on buffets (doubtless a byproduct of its convention business). There is a Friday night all-you-can-eat seafood buffet, a Saturday night all-you-can-eat prime rib buffet, and of course a Sunday all-you-can-eat brunch.

Moderate to expensive. Most dinners $12-19. Serving Sat.-Sun. 7 am-10 pm, Mon.-Fri. 6 am-10 pm. Parking lot. Wheelchair accessible. Smoking & nonsmoking sections. Two cocktail lounges. Children's menu. Children's birthday parties. Seniors discount (age 65+) at all times. Reservations recommended. Catering service. Live piano music daily for lunch & dinner. Dancing Tues.-Sat. Private parties (max. 2,000). All major credit cards. Checks cashed for hotel guests only.

The Village Green
Tavern
7508 Hubbard Ave., Middleton / 608-831-9962
(From University Ave., S on Parmenter St., 2 blks to Hubbard)

Village Green host Ron Boyer and his family dish up burgers, daily specials, Ron's spicy chili, and Wednesday and Friday fish fries. Also featured here is Garten Brau beer, brewed at the Capital Brewery just up the street. The casual atmosphere is accented by historic train memorabillia.

Inexpensive. Most items under $5. Serving Mon.-Sat. from 10 am. Closed Sun. Nearby public parking. Easy curb parking. Dining area wheelchair accessible (but not rest rooms). Bar. Reservations not accepted. Takeouts. Private parties (max. 150). No credit cards. Out-of-town checks OK with ID.

BARABOO
Including Merrimac, Portage, Prairie du Sac, and Reedsburg

The Farm Kitchen
Restaurant / Resort
S5718 Hwy. 123, Baraboo / 608-356-5246
(At the north entrance to Devils Lake State Park)

This is a perfect place for families who are visiting Devils Lake State Park, which is the most popular park in Wisconsin. In addition to the restaurant, there are rental cottages, a swimming pool, a country craft and gift barn, a go-kart track, and a 36-hole miniature golf course. The Farm Kitchen is known for its breakfast buffets, noontime smorgasbord, and Friday evening seafood smorgasbord. The menu carries all the usual supper club fare, including steaks (you can grill your own, if you like), chicken, fish, and seafood. If a family member is having a birthday, be sure to tell the server, and a free birthday cake will be brought in.

Inexpensive to moderate. Most dinners $4.50-11.95. *Summer hours*: Sun. 7:30 am-8:30 pm, Mon.-Sat. 7:30 am-9 pm. *Winter hours*: Fri.-Sat. 11-9, Sun. 7:30 am-8:30 pm. Closed Mon.-Thurs. Parking lot. Wheelchair accessible. Smoking & nonsmoking sections. Full bar. Children's menu. Reservations recommended. Takeouts. Private parties (max. 225). MC, VI, AE. Out-of-town checks OK with ID.

Pierce's Viking II
Supper club
323 South Blvd., Baraboo / 608-356-5122
(Corner of Business 12 & Hwy. 123)

Another popular supper club for those visiting Devils Lake is the venerable Pierce's, located in a historic stone structure, in business since 1929 and under its present ownership since 1978. If you're going out fishing, Pierce's is the perfect place to go for an early breakfast. And, if the rest of the family is back at the cottage sleeping, who's to know if you have a piece of Pierce's delicious home-made pie for breakfast? Pierce's also has a full supper club menu, and is especially proud of its homemade onion rings.

Inexpensive to moderate. Most dinners $7-12. Serving Sun. 7:30-2, weekdays 6 am- 9 pm, Fri.-Sat. 6 am-10 pm. (Breakfast served daily until 11:30 am.) Parking lot. Wheelchair accessible. Smoking & nonsmoking sections. Cocktail lounge/bar. Children's menu. Lighter-eater's menu. Reservations recommended. Takeouts. Private parties (max. 275). MC, VI,DC. No checks.

Susie's
Cafe
146 Fourth Ave., Baraboo / 608-356-9911

Susie's, on the square in historic downtown Baraboo, is a cafe—but what a cafe! Here, you'll find eggs Benedict and Italian frittata at breakfast, chicken quesadillas at lunch, and chicken marsala at dinner. Not quite your usual Wisconsin cafe fare. In his book, *2 to 22 Days Around the Great Lakes*, author Arnold Schuchter called Susie's "the best small gourmet restaurant in the Great Lakes Area"—and we would have a hard time disagreeing. Susie's motto is "A Celebration of Fresh Foods," and its every dish is a living demonstration of that motto. The pastas, the quiches, the stir-fries, the soups and sandwiches, the delicious breakfast buns and desserts—all are homemade. The stir-fries are notable, including one with chicken, cashews, and broccoli; another with tofu, broccoli, and peanut sauce; still another with beef, ginger, and pineapple. The rice-nut salad, with wild rice, cashews, fresh orange slices, almonds, and sunflower seeds, is memorable. The fresh apple pie with cinnamon sauce is worth a special trip. What else can we say about Susie's? It's wonderful. Come.

Inexpensive to moderate. Most dinners $8-12. *Summer hours:* Sun. brunch 8-1:30. Tues.-Sat. 8-2 & 5-8:30. *Winter hours:* Sun. brunch 8-1:30. Tues.-Thurs. 8-1:30. Fri.-Sat., 11-2 & 5-9. Closed Mondays year-round. Dining room wheelchair accessible (but not rest rooms). Totally nonsmoking. Beer & wine served.

Children's menu. Children's birthday parties arranged. Vegetarian entrees. Reservations not accepted. MC, VI. Out-of-town checks OK with ID.

★ ★ ★
The Sandhill Inn
American / regional
170 E. Main St., Merrimac / 608-493-2203
(On Hwy. 78, 5 blks from the Merrimac Ferry)

Here, in a romantic Victorian-style home near the Wisconsin River, is one of the finest restaurants in Wisconsin. The chef is also the co-owner, and he personally prepares almost every dish that comes from the Sandhill kitchen. And some dishes they are! Poached salmon with shiitake mushrooms. Beef tournedos with mushroom duxelle. Lamb chops with brandied lamb sauce. Salmon encroute. Double-chocolate fudge cake. The cuisine at the Sandhill is definitely upscale, but the atmosphere is decidedly unstuffy. There is no dress code, and the service is personal and friendly. The next time you find yourself near Merrimac, and are in the mood for a romantic and elegant dinner, the Sandhill is the place to go.

Moderate to Expensive. Most dinners $13-25. Serving dinner Tues.-Sat. 5:30-10, Sun. brunch 9:30-2. Sun. dinner only in Jun., Jul., & Aug. Easy curb parking. Wheelchair accessible. Smoking & nonsmoking sections. Full bar. Children's portions. Reservations recommended (essential for Sat. dinner). Catering service. Private parties (max. 38). MC, VI, AE. Out-of-town checks OK with ID.

Blankenhaus
Supper club
1223 E. Wisconsin, Portage / 608-742-7555
(On Hwys. 51/16 at the south edge of town)

This popular supper club is operated by Jim and Kay Blankenheim, who took over the restaurant from Jim's parents in 1985. It has long been a popular spot in Portage for weddings, anniversaries, and special occasions—and just for a nice lunch or dinner out, anytime. The Blankenheims serve traditional supper club fare—steaks, chicken, seafood, prime rib, hearty soups, and homemade desserts.

Inexpensive to moderate. Most dinners $7-12. Serving Sun. brunch 11-2, dinner 4:30-10, Tues.-Fri. 11-2 & 4:30-10, Sat. 4:30-10. Closed Mon. Parking lot. Wheelchair accessible. Smoking & nonsmoking sections. Cocktail lounge/bar. Children's portions. Seniors "light" entrees. Reservations recommended. Take-outs. Live organ music & dancing Wed., Fri. & Sun. eves. Private parties (max. 150). MC, VI. Out-of-town checks OK with ID.

Dream Diner
Eclectic / Regional
585 Water St., Prairie du Sac / 608-643-2880
(Downtown, across from the movie theater)

Dan and Janice Ross opened the Dream Diner in 1991, and have been receiving kudos ever since. Chef Dan's experience includes stints at a beachside resort in the Virgin Islands, a Cajun restaurant in Alaska, and some of the best restaurants in Madison. Now, he and Janice have opted for the good life in small-town America. The Dream looks like any other small-town diner, but the menu features specialties such as catfish Creole, beef jardiniere, blackened beefsteak, jambalaya, chicken in Dijon mustard sauce over fettucine, and—the house specialty—Southwestern pecan curry duck. The desserts are wonderful, too, including strawberries in a light caramel glaze. At lunch, the atmosphere is much like that in any other diner, but at dinnertime the emphasis switches to candlelight and romance.

Moderate. Most dinners $10-15. Serving Sun. buffet brunch 9-1. Lunch Wed.-Sat. 11:30-1:30. Dinner Thurs.-Fri.-Sat. 5 to close. Closed Mon. & Tues. Easy curb parking. Not wheelchair accessible. Staff will try to separate nonsmokers from smokers. Beer, wine & specialty drinks served. Reservations recommended (essential for dinner). Reservations not accepted for Sun. brunch. Local deliveries. Takeouts. Catering service. Private parties (max. 35). No credit cards. Out-of-town checks OK with ID.

Voyageur Inn
Supper club
200 Viking Drive, Reedsburg / 608-524-6431
(Corner of Hwy. 33 & Hwy. H)

The Voyageur has been serving local folks since 1972 and has been under its present ownership since 1984. The menu here is standard Wisconsin supper club, with steaks, chicken, barbecue, fish, and seafood specialties. If you can get a windowside table, you'll be soothed by the pine trees and amused by the black and brown squirrels and the birds feeding outside. This is a relaxed place, a good place to bring the children for breakfast, lunch, or dinner.

Inexpensive to moderate. Most dinners $6-15. Serving daily 6:30-2 & 5-9 (Fri. & Sat. until 10). Sun. brunch 8-12:30. Parking lot. Wheelchair accessible. Smoking & nonsmoking sections. Cocktail lounge/bar. Children's menu. Seniors discount. Reservations recommended. Takeouts. Catering service. Private parties (max. 500). MC, VI, AE, Dis. Out-of-town checks OK with ID.

SOUTHEASTERN GATEWAY
Kenosha and Racine

Mangia
Italian
5717 Sheridan Rd., Kenosha / 414-652-4285
(Just S of downtown Kenosha on Hwy. 32)

This true Italian restaurant, opened in 1988, has quickly built a large and dedicated clientele. Owner and head chef Tony Mantuano serves authentic pasta dishes with fish, meat, and vegetables, and, in a large, wood-fired oven, some of the best pizzas this side of Palermo. This is real Italian food, as opposed to Italian-American food. Don't miss it when you are next in the area.

Moderate to expensive. Most dinners $9-20. Serving dinner daily 5-10,lunch Mon.-Fri. only, 11:30-2. Nearby public parking. Wheelchair accessible. Smoking & nonsmoking sections. Cocktail lounge/bar. Children's birthday parties. Reservations recommended (essential on weekends). Takeouts. Catering service. Private parties (max. 120). MC, VI. Out-of-town checks OK with ID.

The Great Wall
Chinese
6025 Washington Ave., Racine / 414-886-9700
(On Hwy. 20, 8 mi E of I-94)

I don't know why it is, but many outstanding Chinese restaurants are located in little strip malls. So it is, here in Racine, where the Great Wall serves some of the best food in the city. The menu shows representative foods from several of China's regions, including some spicy Szechwan dishes, vegetarian specialties from eastern China, and Mongolian beef from the north. Two of the favorite specialties of the house are sesame chicken and moo goo gai pan.

Inexpensive. Most dinners $8-11. Serving Tues.-Thurs. 11-8:30, Fri. 11-9:30, Sat. 4-9:30, Sun. 11-8:30. Closed Mon. Parking lot. Dining area wheelchair accessible (but not rest rooms). Smoking & nonsmoking sections. Cocktail lounge/bar. Children's portions. Reservations recommended. Takeouts. MC, VI, Dis. Out-of-town checks OK with ID.

Main Street Bistro
American with Italian accents
340 Main St., Racine / 414-637-4340
(In downtown Racine)

Here is one of the finest restaurants in the area, located in a former nineteenth-century drug store now turned into a delightful dining spot. The decor is accented with old pharmacy cabinets that hold a beautiful collection of art glass. In a large wood-fired oven, Main Street Bistro turns out great gourmet pizzas, fresh seafood, chicken, lamb, and vegetables. Veal and steaks are expertly grilled and enhanced with Italian seasonings. The desserts here are just as good, so save some room.

Moderate to expensive. Most dinners $9-20. Serving Sun. 11-2:30 (brunch) & 4-9, Mon.-Thurs. 11-2:30 & 5-9:30, Fri. & Sat. 11-2:30 & 5-10:30. Parking lot. Wheelchair accessible. Smoking & nonsmoking sections. Full bar. Children's menu. Children's birthday parties. Reservations essential. Local deliveries. Takeouts. Catering service. MC, VI, AE, DC. No checks.

The Packing House
Supper club
6825 Washington Ave., Racine / 414-886-9866
(On Hwy. 20, E of I-94)

The Packing House, which also has two restaurants in Milwaukee, specializes in steaks, but also has barbecued ribs, seafood, poultry, and veal dishes. It has been under its present ownership since 1974.

Moderate. Most dinners $10-15. Serving Sun. brunch 10-1:30, dinner 4-9. Mon.-Thurs. dinner 5-9, Fri. 4-10, Sat. 5-10. Parking lot. Wheelchair accessible. Smoking & nonsmoking sections. Cocktail lounge/bar. Children's portions. Special "early bird" prices for Fri. fish fry. Seniors discount (age 62+). Reservations recommended. Takeouts. Catering service. Live piano music Fri. & Sat. eves. Private parties (max. 90). All major credit cards. No checks.

Valentyne's
American
1675 Douglas Ave., Racine / 414-633-7500
(Corner of Douglas Ave. & High St.)

Valentyne's is housed in a historic building (1898) full of fine Victorian antiques that the owner, Chris M. Kjaer, has collected from around the world. The atmosphere is romantic, eight dining rooms offering intimate dining experiences. The authentic turn-of-the-century bar features a marble top, carved oak, and decorative brass rails. The Valentyne menu features certified Angus beef, magnificent Australian lobster tail (one-pounders and two-pounders), Chateaubriand, and filet mignon. There is also veal Marsala, beef or veal Oscar, lobster Newburg, chicken cordon bleu, roast rack of lamb, and roast duck. The desserts include cherries jubilee, bananas foster, and strawberries Romanoff. This is one of the most elegant restaurants in the southeast part of the state, perfect for special occasions and for stoking the fires of romance.

Expensive. Most dinners $15-25 (but light dinners $8-12). Serving Sun. 4 to close, Tues.-Fri. 11 to close, Sat. 4 to close. Closed Mon. Parking lot. Wheelchair accessible. Smoking & nonsmoking sections. Cocktail lounge/bar. Small children not encouraged. Reservations recommended. Private parties (max. 60). All major credit cards. No checks.

MILWAUKEE

Beans & Barley Cafe
American / International
1901 E. North Ave., Milwaukee / 414-278-7878
(1-1/2 mi N of downtown; 2-1/2 mi E of I-43)

Home cooking with a vegetarian slant is the strength of Beans & Barley, which has been serving light fare to health-conscious Milwaukeeans since 1973. The homemade soups here are excellent, as are the homemade pastries. Chicken and seafood are also on the menu. Beans & Barley suffered a disastrous fire in the summer of 1993, but loyal patrons rallied to the restoration cause, and we hope that this cafe will be fully operational by the time this book comes off press.

Inexpensive. Most dinners $8-10. Serving Sun. 9-3 (breakfast), Mon.-Thurs. 10-9, Fri. 10-10, Sat. 9 am-10 pm. Parking lot. Wheelchair accessible. Totally nonsmoking. Beer & wine served. Children's portions. Seniors discount every Tues. (age 62+). Reservations not accepted. Local deliveries. Takeouts. Catering service. MC, VI. In-state checks OK with ID.

★ ★ ★
The Boulevard Inn
Continental
Cudahy Tower, 925 E. Wells, Milwaukee / 414-765-1166

This venerable restaurant has been owned and operated by the Strothmann family since 1946. In 1992 it moved from its longtime west side location to the present elegant quarters in the Cudahy towers, overlooking Lake Michigan. German specialties have long been a house staple, but fresh fish now dominates a large section of the menu, fitting in with today's ligher tastes. Other specialties you should try include honey duck (prepared at tableside), Caesar salad, fresh pasta, and wonderful veal dishes. Of course, sauerbraten and wiener schnitzel are still available. This is one of the finest restaurants in Wisconsin, and, since its move, it is also one of the most beautiful.

Expensive. Most dinners $15-25. Serving Sun. 10:30-9 (brunch until 2), weekdays 11:30-9, Fri.-Sat. 11:30-10. Valet parking. Wheelchair accessible. Smoking & nonsmoking sections. Cocktail lounge. Children's menu. A pianist plays contemporary music nightly. Reservations essential. Private parties (max. 60). MC, VI, AE, Dis, DC. No checks.

Elsa's on the Park
American
833 N. Jefferson St., Milwaukee / 414-765-0615

For late-night, light eating, Elsa's is highly recommended. Their sirloin burgers, boneless pork sandwiches, and buffalo wings have satisfied thousands of after-theater patrons since this restaurant's founding in 1980. The menu also offers a salami and cheese plate, Cajun french fries, Greek salad, and nachos. Tempting desserts include cheesecake, strawberry shortcake, chocolate mousse cake, and several sundaes.

Inexpensive. Most platters $4-8. Serving Sun. 5 pm-1 am, Mon.-Fri. 11 am-1 am, Sat. 5 pm-1 am. Nearby public parking. Curb parking. Wheelchair accessible. No policy on smoking. Full bar. Small children not encouraged. Reservations not accepted. Takeouts. No credit cards. Out-of-town checks OK with ID.

★ ★ ★
The English Room at The Pfister Hotel
Continental
424 E. Wisconsin Ave., Milwaukee / 414-273-8222

The Pfister, opened in 1893, is the most famous hotel in Milwaukee, and the elegant English Room has been its shining centerpiece since 1926. The specialty of the house is roast rack of lamb Provencal, and the menu also offers a large selection of other Continental dishes—veal, beef, poultry, and seafood. The decor is formal, with an authentic nineteenth-century art collection. This is a most romantic restaurant, a favorite place for anniversaries and special occasions for generations of Milwaukeeans.

Expensive. Most dinners $17-27. Serving Sun. 5-10, Mon.-Fri. 11:30-2 & 5:30-11, Sat. 5:30-11. Parking ramp. Wheelchair accessible. Smoking & nonsmoking sections. Cocktail lounge/bar. Small children not encouraged. Reservations essential. Live harp music Mon.-Sat. eves. Private parties (max. 24). All major credit cards.

★ ★ ★
Grenadier's
Continental / French
747 N. Broadway St., Milwaukee / 414-276-0747

Milwaukee has been totally in love with Grenadier's since it opened in 1975. German-born owner and chef Knut Apitz trained in Europe and cooked for the Holland America Cruise Line before coming to Milwaukee. The menu is strongly Continental, but Apitz is not afraid to bring in other influences in exercising his culinary creativity. Thus the menu features specialties such as pork tenderloin with pfifferlinge and spaetzle, Texas wild boar in pistachio and walnut crust, braised shank of Scottish wild hare, fresh Norwegian salmon stuffed with smoked salmon, filet mignon in peppercorn crust on roasted garlic sauce, and fresh Maryland crabcakes. Hors d'oeuvres include such imaginative creations as blue corn crepes with goat cheese, fresh lump crabmeat on Belgian endive with English mustard sauce, and terrine and grilled breast of duck with cumberland sauce. Of course, there are house specials every evening, giving further vent to Knut Apitz's extraordinary imagination. This is certainly one of the very best restaurants in Wisconsin, a true dining experience.

Expensive. Most dinners $16-22. Serving Mon.-Fri. 10:30-2:30 & 5:30-10. Sat. dinner 5:30-10:30. Closed Sun. Parking lot. Wheelchair accessible. Smoking & nonsmoking sections. Cocktail lounge/bar. Small children not encouraged. Reservations recommended. Catering service. Live piano music every evening. Private parties (max. 42). All major credit cards. Out-of-town checks OK with ID.

Hook's Bar & Grill
American
1110 N. Old World St., Milwaukee / 414-272-2333
(Corner of Highland & 3rd St., 1 blk E of Bradley Center)

We feel this is one of the best places to go before or, especially, after a sporting event at the Bradley Center—hockey, basketball, or soccer. The menu is loaded with hearty sandwiches, soups, salads, and super snacks. Some specialties include jambalaya, German pizza, a double Reuben, barbecued beef, Italian salami sandwich, brats, smoked Polish sausage, chili, seafood chowder, Sicilian salad, Bavarian bean soup, oysters on the half shell, cheese head marinara (fried cheese), Door County cherry pie, frozen peanut butter pie, cheesecake, and apple strudel. All this and large-screen TV mean that you don't even have to go to the Bradley Center. Just stay here, snack, and watch the game on TV. Save yourself a bundle. (There is also a great Friday night fish fry.)

Inexpensive. Most items $5-7. Serving daily 11 am-midnight. Parking lot. Wheelchair accessible. No policy on smoking. Bar. Children's portions. Reservations not accepted. Takeouts. Catering service. Live jazz Sat. eve. MC, VI, AE. Out-of-town checks OK with ID.

Jack Pandl's Whitefish Bay Inn
American
1319 E. Henry Clay St., Milwaukee / 414-964-3800
(Lake Drive at 5200 N)

This is a true Milwaukee institution, serving local burghers since 1915. The restaurant still retains an old-time Milwaukee atmosphere, and claims the largest public display of antique beer steins in the U.S.A. Pandl's is famous for its German pancakes, a tempting entry for Sunday brunchers. (This was voted best Sunday brunch in town by readers of *Milwaukee* magazine.) Other house specialties are the fresh broiled and boned whitefish and roast Wisconsin duck with sage dressing. Other menu items include walleye pike, wiener schnitzel, veal liver, catfish (also boned), broiled lamb chops, steaks, pork chops, and barbecued ribs. There is a good selection of German beers on tap to wash it all down. Special homemade desserts include chocolate mousse, pecan pie, and strawberry schaum torte. All this is served at modest prices in a relaxed atmosphere.

Moderate. Most dinners $10-15. Serving Sun. 10-2 & 4-8, Mon.-Thurs. 11:30-2:30 & 5-9, Fri.-Sat. 11:30-2:30 & 5-11. Parking lot. Not wheelchair accessible. Smoking & nonsmoking sections. Cocktail lounge/bar. Children's birthday parties. Children's menu. Reservations recommended. Takeouts. All major credit cards. No checks.

John Ernst Cafe
German
600 E. Ogden, Milwaukee / 414-273-1878

This is the oldest restaurant in Milwaukee, founded in 1878. John and Ida Ernst acquired the place in 1938, and now the second and third generations of the family, led by Marianne and Ervin Lindenberg, carry on the fine tradition of German cuisine and hospitality. Diners here will be enveloped in a romantic, old world atmosphere, highlighted by a beautiful fireplace. Old world specialties on the menu include beef rouladen, wiener schnitzel, sauerbraten, kassler rippen (smoked pork chops), veal goulash, pork shank with sauerkraut, and bratwursts. There is also a full menu of American dishes—prime rib, steaks, roast turkey, lamb chops, Dover sole, shrimp, scallops, lobster tail, and soft-shell crabs. There is also a "petite fare" section of the menu, for those without old world appetites.

Moderate to expensive. Most dinners $11-17. Serving Sun. noon-9:30, Tues.-Sat. 11:45-10:30. Closed Mon. Parking lot. Wheelchair accessible. Smoking & non-smoking sections. Full bar. Children's menu. Reservations recommended. Take-outs. Live dinner music nightly. Private parties (max. 125). All major credit cards. No checks.

Karl Ratzsch's Old World Restaurant
German / Continental
320 E. Mason St., Milwaukee / 414-276-2720
(4 blks from I-43, Broadway exit)

This is one of the famous old German restaurants that helped to make Milwaukee famous, and vice versa. The establishment dates back to 1904 and has undergone a move and a couple of name changes since then, but has been Karl Ratzsch's for more than sixty years, now, and in fact has been run by a Karl Ratzsch all that time (The present owner is Karl Ratzsch III). As always, the menu leans toward hearty German dishes. For appetizers, try Koenigsberger klopse, beef rouladen, goose liver pate, or smoked pork, cheese and sauerkraut in pastry. Traditional entrees include sauerbraten, roast goose shank, roast duck, braised lamb shank, stuffed or smoked pork chops, Rheinlander schnitzel, or wiener schnitzel. There are also some tempting fish and seafood entrees and some nice potato and vegetable side dishes. Bring your appetite to Karl Ratzsch's.

Expensive. Most dinners $17-22. Serving Sun. 11-10 (brunch 11-3), Mon.-Fri. 11:30-10, Sat. 11:30-11:30. Valet parking at dinner. Not wheelchair accessible. Smoking & nonsmoking sections. Full bar. Children's menu. Children's birthday parties. Reservations recommended. Live piano music nightly. Private parties (max. 55). All major credit cards. No checks.

The King and I
Thai
833 N. Second St., Milwaukee / 414-276-4181

This is an authentic Thai restaurant in downtown Milwaukee. The menu offers a wide variety of beef, chicken, and seafood entrees, each custom-spiced according to the customer's preference for hotness. Specialties here include Panang Nau, "King and I" fried rice, crispy duck or pineapple duck, and volcano chicken. There are also some notable appetizers and desserts, all bringing the special flavors and textures of Thai cuisine to the Beer City.

Moderate. Most dinners $10-15. Serving Sun. 4-7, Mon.-Fri. 11:30-10, Sat. 5-11. Parking lot. Wheelchair accessible. Smoking & nonsmoking sections. Cocktail lounge/bar. Children's birthday parties. Reservations recommended. Takeouts. Catering service. Private parties (max. 50). All major credit cards. No checks.

Mader's
German
1037-41 N. Third St., Milwaukee
414-271-3377 or 1-800-558-7171

Mader's is one of the most famous German restaurants in America, a landmark in downtown Milwaukee since 1902. The restaurant is located in a sprawling structure that resembles a Medieval castle, and is still owned and operated by the Mader family after more than 90 years. The family's art collection, consisting mainly of Medieval antiques and wildlife prints, has grown so large that, in 1989, a separate art gallery was started, just south of the restaurant. Mader's is enormously popular with tourists, who flock here as much for the spectacular old world atmosphere as for the food, which, in these days of light dining, is less popular than it was when horse-drawn wagons hauled wooden barrels of beer through Milwaukee's streets. The menu is extraordinary, including, for just one example, 32 cold appetizers. Specialties among entrees include roast pork shank, sauerbraten, roast duck, various wursts, rippchen, Hungarian goulash, beef rouladen, sauerkraut, and eight veal (schnitzel) dishes. There are wonderful cheesecakes and apple strudel for dessert, and, of course, Black Forest torte. In both atmosphere and cuisine, Mader's is an absolutely overwhelming dining experience. On a visit to Milwaukee, everyone should have that experience at least once. (Mader's is one block east of the Bradley Center, home of the Milwaukee Bucks.)

Moderate to expensive. Most dinners $14-22. Serving lunch Mon.-Sat. 11:30-4. Dinner weekdays & Sun. until 10:30, Fri.-Sat. until 11:30. Sun. brunch 10:30-3. Valet parking. Wheelchair accessible. Smoking & nonsmoking sections. Cocktail lounge. Children's menu. Reservations recommended. Private parties (max. 110). All major credit cards.

Marangelli's Al Lago
Continental / Italian
777 E. Michigan, Milwaukee / 414-272-0777

This romantic, upscale Italian restaurant is located on the galleria level of the tallest Milwaukee skyscraper (Firstar) to face Lake Michigan. Here, you can get a splendid view of the lake. Marangelli's is a new restaurant, opened in the spring of 1993. The decor is modern and stylish, and the lounge is *trés* romantic. The cuisine here is in the Northern Italian style, featuring seasonal creative specialties, vegetable dishes, pasta, seafood, meats, poultry, and game. Some specialties include Cappuccini E Fettuccine—seared medallion of tenderloin with brandied coffee wine glaze, served with fettucine—and Rondelle Di Salmone—scallops of Norwegian salmon charred with basil oil and roasted oyster in spinach wrapping. Chef John G. Marangelli presides.

Expensive. Most dinners $16-24. Serving luncheon Mon.-Fri. (hours not given), dinner weekdays 5-10, Fri. 5-11, Sat. 5-close. Free underground parking in evening. Wheelchair accessible. Smoking not encouraged. Full bar. Lounge. Children's portions. Reservations recommended. Takeouts on request. Private parties (max. 40). MC, VI, AE. Some checks OK with ID.

Mimma's Cafe
Italian
1307 E. Brady St., Milwaukee / 414-271-7337
(3 blks W of Lake Michigan & 10 blks N of Wisconsin Ave.)

Mimma's is located on historic Brady Street. The exterior of the building was restored to its 1865 appearance after the restaurant's founding in 1989, and the interior has been done in an elegant black and white motif. This is one of the trendy restaurants in Milwaukee today, a place to see and be seen. Specialties of the house include seafood pasta dishes, grilled fresh fish, and more than fifty different pasta dishes (*Milwaukee* magazine readers voted this the best pasta restaurant in town). There are also nightly specials.

Expensive. Most dinners $25-30. Serving Sun. 4-10, Tues.-Thurs. 11-3 & 5-11, Fri. 11-3 & 5-midnight, Sat. noon-3 & 5-midnight. Parking is difficult. Wheelchair accessible. Smoking OK in bar, not in dining room. Cocktail lounge/bar. Reservations recommended for lunch. Reservations not accepted for dinner. Catering service. MC, VI, AE, Dis. Out-of-town checks OK with ID.

Pandl's in Bayside
American
8825 N. Lake Dr., Milwaukee / 414-352-7300

This attractive east Milwaukee restaurant features a dining room completely surrounded by large windows looking out onto a wilderness area. Many species of birds and other wildlife can be seen at certain times of day. Pandl's menu features fresh seafood of many kinds, and the Sunday brunch is said to be outstanding.

Expensive. Most dinners $15-20. Serving weekdays 11:30-2 & 5-9:30, Fri.-Sat. 11:30-2 & 5-10:30, Sun. brunch 10:30-2, dinner 4-9. Parking lot. Wheelchair accessible. Smoking & nonsmoking sections. Cocktail lounge. Children's menu. Reservations recommended. Takeouts. Catering service. Private parties (max. 200). All major credit cards.

The Pasta Tree
Continental / Italian
1503 N. Farwell Ave., Milwaukee / 414-276-8867
(1-1/2 blks from the lakefront)

This restaurant has been voted "best romantic pasta restaurant" by readers of Milwaukee's *Shepherd Express.* The specialties here are in keeping with today's emphasis on light eating and moderate waistlines—fresh fish with pasta.

Moderate. Most dinners $9-15. Serving Sun. 5-9, Mon.-Thurs. 11:30-2:30 & 4-9, Fri. 11:30-2:30 & 4-10, Sat. 11:30-10. Parking lot. Dining room wheelchair accessible (but not rest rooms). Totally nonsmoking. Beer & wine served. Small children not encouraged. Reservations not accepted. Takeouts. Catering service. MC, VI. Out-of-town checks OK with ID.

Pieces of Eight
American
550 N. Harbor Dr., Milwaukee / 414-271-0597

This is Milwaukee's only lakefront restaurant, specializing in fresh seafood, prime rib, and a gourmet salad bar.

Moderate to expensive. Most dinners $11-23. Serving Sun. 9:30-2 (brunch) & 4-10, Mon.-Thurs. 11-3 & 4:30-10, Fri.-Sat. 11-3 & 4:30-11. Parking lot. Wheelchair accessible. Smoking & nonsmoking sections. Cocktail lounge/bar. Patio. Reservations recommended. All major credit cards. No checks.

Sanford
French / New American
1547 N. Jackson St., Milwaukee / 414-276-9608

This is a fairly new restaurant (founded 1989) but has already gained a reputation as one of Milwaukee's finest. It is located in the former Sanford family grocery store, in the family for 75 years. Owner Sanford D'Amato, who runs the restaurant with his wife, Angie, is one of Milwaukee's most talented chefs. He serves a variety of Continental and American dishes. Some specialties are: savory cumin wafers with grilled rare tuna and cilantro dressing; seared tournados of sea scallops with crispy noodles and curry vinaigrette; and char-grilled duck with green olive and eggplant compote. The desserts are also outstanding. In fact, *Milwaukee* magazine readers voted them best in town. Sanford's offers a dining experience not to be missed.

Expensive. Most dinners $20-30. Serving dinner weekdays 5:30-9, Fri.-Sat. until 10. Closed Sun. Valet parking. Wheelchair accessible. Totally nonsmoking. Extensive wine list. Children not encouraged. Reservations recommended. MC, VI, AE, Dis, DC. Out-of-town checks OK with ID.

Saz's State House
American
5539 W. State St., Milwaukee / 414-453-2410
(10 blks W of Miller Brewing)

Say "Saz" to many Milwaukeeans and they will think of two things—barbecued ribs and Milwaukee Brewer baseball. This famous restaurant is mobbed before Brewer games, and everybody seems to be having a good time. The restaurant runs buses to County Stadium for the games, and also arranges high-class tailgate parties for groups. Saz's also run buses to the Bradley Center for basketball and hockey games. The big draw inside the restaurant is the ribs, which are some of the best in the Midwest, annually voted best in Milwaukee. You can get a full order or a half order of pork ribs, or you can choose beef ribs or even barbecued chicken. How about chicken 'n ribs, or shrimp 'n ribs, lasagna 'n ribs, or even pork 'n beef ribs mixed—you get the idea. Other items on the menu include chicken parmesan, orange roughy almondine, lemon-tarragon chicken, and Sicilian steak. Friday nights brings beer batter cod, fresh lake perch, fish 'n ribs (why not?), and clam chowder. Saz's also has sandwiches on the dinner menu, and a full lunch menu. The food here is great, the prices reasonable, and the service friendly. Everybody loves Saz's (which also has restaurants in the Grand Avenue Mall and in Waukesha).

Moderate. Most dinners $8-15. Serving Sun. 10:30-2:30 (Southwest-style brunch) & 3:30-10, other days 11-11. Parking lot. Wheelchair accessible. Smoking & nonsmoking sections. 2 bars. Children's menu. Local deliveries. Takeouts. Catering service. Singing machine Thurs. eve. Private dining room (max. 40). MC, VI, AE.

Trattoria 631
Italian
631 E. Chicago St., Milwaukee / 414-223-2180
(Corner of Jackson St., 1 blk W of main gates of Summerfest grounds)

Trattoria 631 is the sleek cafe of the new Italian Community Center, which opened in 1990. The dining room is flanked by two walls of floor-to-ceiling windows. One looks out onto the boccie courts, the other onto an outdoor dining area. The small kitchen, open to public view, is located just behind the u-shaped bar. Here, you will find authentic Italian foods from all the regions of the old country—butter and cream dishes of the north, fish of the coasts, tomato-based pasta and olive oil specialties of the south. Menu items are rotated periodically, so that all of Italy's twenty regions are represented at least some of the time—a wise policy for a restaurant manager who represents the entire Italian community of Milwaukee. Specialties we have enjoyed in the past include penne rigatoni (Italian sausage with broccoli, tomato, garlic, herbs, and Parmesan cheese), veal with a porcini mushroom cream sauce over linguine, and char-grilled sole with steamed spinach, grilled red pepper strips, and fava beans. For real Italian food, you couldn't do better.

Inexpensive to moderate. Most dinners $5-15. Serving lunch Mon.-Fri. 11-2:30. Dinner Wed.-Thurs. 5-9, Fri.-Sat. 5-10. Closed Sun. Parking lot. Wheelchair accessible. Bar in dining area. Reservations recommended. Takeouts. Catering service. Private dining room (max. 700). MC, VI, AE. Out-of-town checks OK with ID.

Weissgerber's Third Street Pier
Continental / German / Seafood
1110 Old World Third St., Milwaukee / 414-272-0330
(Corner of Highland & Third Sts.)

Here is a romantic restaurant located right on the Milwaukee River, offering a great view of the water and the city skyline. The Third Street Pier is known especially for seafood and steak, but other entrees include pasta dishes, poultry, and veal. Seafood entrees include Caribbean bouillabaisse, Dover sole, shrimp Provencale, seafood Linguine, swordfish, orange roughy, and Cajun catfish. There is a Friday fish fry "par excellence" and more than two hundred wines from which to choose.

Expensive. Most dinners $15-25. Serving Sun. 4-9, Mon.-Fri. 11:30-2 & 5-10, Sat. 5-10. Valet parking (or park at Bradley Center lot). Wheelchair accessible. Smoking & nonsmoking sections. Cocktail lounge/bar. Reservations recommended. Live classical piano music Tues.-Sun. eves. Private parties (max. 200). MC, VI, AE. Out-of-town checks OK with ID.

WEST OF MILWAUKEE

Including Cedarburg, Elm Grove, Fox Point, Glendale, Hartland, Hubertus, Mequon, Mukwonago, Nashotah, New Berlin, Oconomowoc, Okauchee, Pewaukee, Waukesha, and West Bend

Barth's at the Bridge
American / German
N58 W6194 Columbia Rd., Cedarburg / 414-377-0660
(On Hwy. 57 in downtown Cedarburg)

This is a truly fine, old restaurant in a most charming town, run by the same family for more than fifty years. The building, like many in Cedarburg, is on the National Register of Historic Places. Cozy, candlelit dining rooms and the cocktail lounge are decorated with antiques and works of local artists. Specialties include homemade soups, roast prime rib, beef Wellington, and German schnitzels. Desserts feature homemade pecan pie and strawberry schaum torte. The most popular lunch item is Barth's famous Whitehouse Sandwich. The restaurant tends to draw big crowds for Sunday brunch and the Friday night seafood buffet, so be sure to make reservations at these times. Barth's at the Bridge is highly recommended for dependable and satisfying dining.

Moderate. Most dinners $11-15. Serving Sun. brunch 10-2, dinner 4-8. Weekdays & Sat. lunch 11-4, dinner 4-9 (Fri. until 10). Closed Mon. Parking lot. Wheelchair accessible. Smoking & nonsmoking sections. Cocktail lounge/bar. Children's menu. "Early bird" prices on Fri. seafood buffet. Reservations recommended. Private parties (max. 30). MC, VI, AE, DC, CB. Out-of-town checks OK with ID.

Elm Grove Inn
Continental / Seafood
13275 Watertown Plank Rd., Elm Grove / 414-782-7090
(From I-94, N on Moorland Rd., E on Watertown Plank Rd. to restaurant)

This is believed to be the oldest continually operating restaurant in Wisconsin, founded in 1855, when Franklin Pierce was president. The two dining rooms are decorated in a Williamsburg motif, both with fireplaces. The menu lists many Continental dishes, centering on veal, fresh fish, lamb, and fish. The atmosphere here is warm and inviting, and the service is friendly and efficient.

Expensive. Most dinners $15-22. Serving Mon.-Sat. 11:30-2 & 5-9:30. Closed Sun. Parking lot. Wheelchair accessible. Smoking & nonsmoking sections. Cocktail lounge/bar. Small children not encouraged. Reservations recommended. Catering service. Private parties (max. 45). MC, VI, AE. Out-of-town checks OK with ID.

Pizzeria Uno
Italian / Cafe
15280 W. Bluemound Rd., Elm Grove / 414-821-1755
(From I-94, N on Moorland Rd., R on Bluemound Rd. 1 blk on left)

Pizzeria Uno has ties going clear back to the famous Chicago Pizzeria Uno, founded by Ike Sewell. This Uno opened in 1991 and carries on the fine tradition. Featuring a beautiful full-service bar, large exterior windows, and spacious seating, Uno's Milwaukee restaurant is light, sunny, and festive during lunch, cozy, warm, and relaxed in the evening. The star attraction here, of course, is Chicago-style deep-dish pizza. but there are also other Italian-style dishes on the menu, along with salads and side dishes. This is a fun place to go for great pizza, and you can take the kids.

Inexpensive. Most dinners $6-9. Serving daily from 11 am. Parking lot. Wheelchair accessible. Smoking and nonsmoking sections. Cocktail lounge/bar. Children's menu. Children's birthday parties. Reservations not accepted. Local deliveries. Takeouts. Private parties (max. 45). MC, VI, AE, Dis. Out-of-town checks OK with ID.

Maniaci's Cafe Siciliano
Italian / Continental
6904 N. Santa Monica Blvd., Fox Point / 414-352-5757
(From I-43, exit Good Hope Rd. to Port Washington Rd., 1 blk S
to Green Tree, L on Green Tree 3 blks to Santa Monica,
R into shopping center)

Maniaci's has been serving fine Italian cuisine since 1976 to an appreciative and loyal clientele. Generous portions are served at this restaurant. Dinner entrees include antipasto, soup, salad, potato or pasta, bread, and beverage. Maniaci's turns out wonderful dishes of veal, fresh fish, and, of course, many pasta specialties. There are also great desserts. The atmosphere is cozy at this owner/chef operated restaurant.

Moderate to Expensive. Most dinners $15-25. Serving Mon.-Sat. 4-10 pm. Closed Sun. Parking lot. Not wheelchair accessible. Smoking & nonsmoking sections. Reservations recommended. MC, VI, AE.

Bavarian Inn
German supper club
700 W. Lexington Ave., Glendale / 414-964-0300
(Call for directions)

There are many German specialties at this old-time supper club, now more than half a century under the same ownership. Especially popular are the Friday night fish fry and the Sunday brunch.

Inexpensive to moderate. Most dinners $8-14. Serving Sun. 10:30-2 (brunch) & 4:30-9, Mon.-Thurs. 11:30-9, Fri. 11:30-10, Sat. 5-9. Parking lot. Wheelchair accessible. No policy on smoking. Cocktail lounge/bar. Children's menu. Children's birthday parties. Seniors discount every Tues. (age 65+). Reservations recommended. Takeouts. Catering service. Private parties (max. 500). MC, VI, AE, Dis, DC. Out-of-town checks OK with ID.

Sanidas Cobblestone Inn
Supper club
122 E. Capitol Dr., Hartland / 414-367-8270
(From Hwy. 16, S on Merton Ave., W on Capitol Dr.)

This supper club, located in a historic building called Sign of the Willows, was established in 1929 and has been under present ownership since 1989. It specializes in ribs, veal, lamb, and Greek dishes. There is outdoor dining on the deck in summer, where patrons can get a grand view of the Bark River.

Moderate. Most dinners $10-18. Serving Sun. 3-9, Mon.-Thurs. 11-10, Fri. 11-11, Sat. 4-11. Limited parking. Nearby public parking. Not wheelchair accessible. No policy on smoking. Cocktail lounge/bar. Children's portions on some items. Special "early bird" prices Fri. 4-5:30. Reservations recommended. Takeouts. Catering service. Private parties (max. 90). MC, VI, AE. Out-of-town checks OK with ID.

Weissgerber's Seven Seas
Supper club
1807 Nagawicka Rd., Hartland / 414-367-3903
(From I-94, N on Hwy. 83 1 mi to Nagawicka Rd., turn L)

This scenic restaurant occupies a building that began as a resort, in 1902. The present restaurant has been operating since 1961 and under present ownership since 1981. The setting, overlooking Lake Nagawicka, a popular sailing lake, is a beautiful one. In winter, patrons can cozy up to the fireplace in the main dining room. There is a full menu of supper club selections, but the house specialties are seafood, prime rib, and veal. There are also nightly specials. Especially popular is the Sunday champagne brunch.

Moderate to expensive. Most dinners $12-20. Serving Sun. 11-2 (brunch) & 4-9, Mon.-Sat. dinner 5-10. Closed Tues. in winter. Parking lot. Dining area wheelchair accessible (but not rest rooms). Smoking & nonsmoking sections. Cocktail lounge/bar. Children's portions. Reservations recommended. Catering service. Private parties (max. 180). MC, VI, AE, DC. Out-of-town checks OK with ID.

Anderson's
American
1474 E. Friess Lake Dr., Hubertus / 414-628-3718

Located on the shore of Friess Lake, in the Holy Hill area, Anderson's offers great views of the surrounding Kettle Moraine country. Begin with cocktails on the restaurant's deck (weather and season permitting), then move inside to enjoy fresh fish and seafood, steaks, veal, lamb, pork, and other items from the extensive menu. Many local people hold wedding parties and other events outdoors on the lakefront.

Moderate. Most dinners $12-15. Serving dinner Tues.-Sat. 5-9:30. Sun. brunch 11-2, dinner 4-8. Closed Mon. Closed Tues. Nov. through Apr. Parking lot. Wheelchair accessible. No policy on smoking. Cocktail lounge. Children's portions. Reservations recommended. Takeouts. Catering service. Private parties on lakefront. MC, VI, DC, CB.

★ ★ ★
Fox & Hounds
American / German
1298 Friess Lake Rd., Hubertus / 414-251-4100
(Hwy. 45 N of Milwaukee, W on Hwy. 167/Holy Hill Rd. 6.5 mi,
S on Friess Lake Rd. 1 mi)

The Fox & Hounds is located in the scenic Kettle Moraine country, just two miles from Holy Hill. The sprawling restaurant occupies a rustic log building that, with seven working fireplaces, imparts a cozy north woods atmosphere. The original building dates back to 1832, but has been altered and enlarged many times. This is a wonderful place to come to eat, summer or winter, one of our favorites in the Milwaukee area. Specialties of the house include roast goose breast or shank, stuffed pork chops, cold water lobster tail, prime rib, and great steaks. The spinach salad is highly recommended, and all the desserts and soups are home-made. There are 80 beers and 600 wines on the list. The Fox & Hounds also has one of the most sumptuous Sunday brunches around. For real country dining, this is a great place.

Expensive. Most dinners $15-22. Serving Sun. 10:30-1:30 (brunch) & 2-9, Tues.-Fri. 5-9:30, Sat. until 10. Closed Mon. Parking lot. Wheelchair accessible. Smoking & nonsmoking sections (but moving toward totally nonsmoking). Cocktail lounge/bar. Children's menu. Reservations strongly recommended. Takeouts. Catering service. Private parties (max. 130). All major credit cards. Wisconsin checks OK with ID.

Boder's on the River
American
11919 N. River Rd., Mequon / 414-242-0335
(Call for directions)

This is one of the best known and most popular restaurants in the Milwaukee area. Founded in 1929 by Mr. & Mrs. John Boder, as a tea shop, it has gradually evolved into a full-service restaurant, now run by the third generation of the Boder family. In charming surroundings, the specialties here include roast Wisconsin duckling, baked whitefish, fresh chicken livers with mushrooms, veal, and stuffed rainbow trout. Boder's makes all their own mayonnaise and honey dressings, cherry and blueberry muffins, corn fritters, a variety of tortes and pies, and relishes and soups. They also serve a fresh fruit tray instead of a vegetable salad with all dinners. Complete dinners also come with dessert and beverage (so there's no getting out of eating dessert!).

Moderate to expensive. Most dinners $11-20. Serving Sun. 11:30-2 (brunch & full menu) & 4-7, Tues.-Thurs. 11:30-2 & 5:30-8, Fri. 11:30-2 & 5-8:30, Sat.

11:30-2 & 5:30-9. Closed Mon. Parking lot. Wheelchair accessible. Smoking & nonsmoking sections. Cocktail lounge/bar. Children's menu. Special "early bird" prices Fri. only. Reservations recommended. Private parties. All major credit cards. Out-of-town checks OK with ID.

Chip and Py's
Continental
1340 W. Towne Square Rd., Mequon / 414-241-9589

Chip and Py's serves a largely Italian/French menu, with just a touch of Thai influence, resulting in dishes such as shrimp Sriracha, steak au poivre, Masaman beef, veal piccatta, Sicilian steak sandwich, and Thai beef salad. To this eclectic mix, throw in several Cajun dishes and you've got yourself a fascinating melange. This cozy restaurant features a fire- place, a large wine list by the glass, and a jazz duo that plays on Wednes- day, Friday, and Saturday nights.

Moderate. Most dinners $9-14. "Early bird" prices. Serving Sun. 4-9, weekdays 11:30-2 & 5-10, Fri until 11, Sat. 11:30-2:30 & 4:30-11. Off-street parking. Wheelchair accessible. Smoking & nonsmoking sections. Cocktail lounge. Small children not encouraged. Private parties (max. 70). All major credit cards. Out-of-town checks OK with ID.

★ ★ ★

The Riversite
Regional American
11120 N. Cedarburg Rd., Mequon / 414-242-6050
(SE corner Hwys. 57 & 167, 3 mi W of I-43 on Mequon Rd.167)

This elegant and popular restaurant has been building a steady clientele since its founding by Jim Marks in 1988. From their tables overlooking the Milwaukee River, patrons can often see wildlife cavorting on the grounds outside. The cuisine here, which is not only excellently prepared but also beautifully presented, encourages heart-healthy dining, with fresh seafood and fish, wild game, lean meats, and—as a reward—beautiful chocolate desserts. The atmosphere is casual and relaxed at the Riversite, but the creative cuisine is among the very best in Wisconsin.

Expensive. Most dinners $15-20. Serving Mon.-Fri. 5-10 pm, Sat. 5-11. Closed Sun. Parking lot. Wheelchair accessible. Smoking & nonsmoking sections. Cocktail lounge/bar. Children's portions on request. Reservations recommended (essential on weekends). Takeouts. Catering service. Private parties (max. 50). MC, VI, AE, DC, CB. Out-of-town checks OK with ID.

★ ★ ★

Heaven City
American
S91 W27850 Hwy ES, Mukwonago / 414-363-5191
(Call for directions)

Heaven City is located in a 1917 Frank Lloyd Wright-style building, with art deco leaded glass and inlaid floors throughout. It has been voted one of the most romantic restaurants in the state. (Its notorious past includes gangster connections in the 1930s.) In this character-laden building, Heaven City serves up some very tasty specialties, including smoked trout turnovers, mushroom-brie tart, chicken breast filled with smoked barbecue and brick cheese, and roast duckling with Door County cherry, port wine, and orange sauce. For dessert, how about apple tart with caramel sauce, peach cobbler, or Irish coffec? Heaven City, indeed.

Moderate to expensive. Most dinners $10-18. Serving Sun. 5-9. Lunch Mon.-Fri. 11:30-2. Dinner Mon.-Sat. 5:30-10. Parking lot. Not wheelchair accessible. No smoking in dining room. Smoking OK in cocktail lounge/bar. Reservations recommended (essental on weekends). Catering service. Live jazz Fri.-Sat.-Sun. eves. Private parties (max. 36). MC, VI, AE, DC. Out-of-town checks OK with ID.

★ ★ ★

Red Circle Inn
American
N44 W33013 Watertown Plank Rd., Nashotah / 414-367-4883
(From I-94, Exit #285 4 mi N on Hwy. C to Watertown Plank Rd.)

The Red Circle has a long history, beginning in 1848 as a stagecoach stop and hotel for travelers, later serving as an oasis for wealthy city people living or summering in Wisconsin's "lake country." The Pabst family (of brewing fame) owned the inn for a time, and it was Captain Pabst who named it the Red Circle, after one of his beer labels. The menu features fresh fish, beef, veal, lamb, and poultry dishes. Wonderful appetizers and desserts are also available. This is a beautiful country restaurant, offering a warm and comfortable dining experience long to be remembered.

Moderate to expensive. Most dinners $15-20. Serving Tues.-Sat. 5-9:30. Closed Sun. & Mon. Parking lot. Wheelchair accessible. Smoking and nonsmoking sections. Cocktail lounge/bar. Reservations recommended (essential on weekends). Private parties (max. 250). MC, VI, AE. Out-of-town checks OK with ID.

Alida's Alpine Inn
German// American
16150 W. National Ave., New Berlin / 414-784-6359

This restaurant, serving many German specialties and American dishes, has been operating since 1979.

Moderate. Most dinners $9-13. Serving Tues.-Thurs. 11-2 & 4:30-9, Fri. 4-10, Sat. 4:30-10, Sun. 4-9. Closed Mon. Parking lot. Wheelchair accessible. Smoking & nonsmoking sections. Cocktail lounge. Children's menu. Children's birthday parties. Seniors discount (65). Takeouts. Catering service. Private parties (max. 120). All major credit cards. No checks.

Bartlett's
Supper club
1508 W. National Ave., New Berlin / 414-782-6260
(Corner of Moorland Rd. & National Ave.)

Bartlett's specializes in succulent prime rib, tender veal dishes, fresh fish and seafood, and of course the traditional Friday fish fry. The atmosphere is relaxed and the staff is most friendly. Kids are always welcome.

Moderate. Most dinners $8-16. Serving Mon.-Thurs. 11-2 & 4-10, Fri. 11-10:30, Sat. 4-10:30. Closed Sun. Parking lot. Wheelchair accessible. Smokers and non-smokers are separated on request. Cocktail lounge/bar. Light menu Mon.-Thurs. eves. Reservations recommended, essential on weekends. Takeouts. Live entertainment nightly. Small dance floor. Private parties (max. 250). MC, VI, AE, Dis. No checks.

★ ★ ★

Steven Wade's Cafe
American
17001 W. Greenfield Ave., New Berlin / 414-784-0774
(From Moorland Rd., W on Greenfield Ave. to 170th St.)

This romantic restaurant has been owned and operated since 1986 by Steven and Judy Klindt, in a 1917 house in Waukesha County. Steven, who is also the chief chef, changes the menu daily, taking advantage of each day's prime food offerings. Dennis Getto, restaurant critic of the *Milwaukee Journal*, was especially taken by one of Steven's creations, Crab Soup East-West, combining West Coast Dungeness crab with East Coast lumpfin crab in a sauce of stock and fresh cream. Each dish here is a result of Steven Klindt's special creative touch, each cooked to order. This is one of the finest restaurants in the state, well worth a special visit.

Expensive. Most dinners $19-27. Serving Sun. 4:30-8:30, Mon.-Fri. 11:30-2 & 5:30-10, Sat. 5:30-10. Parking lot. Wheelchair accessible. Smoking & nonsmoking sections. Small bar. Reservations recommended. Takeouts. Private dining room (max. 8). All major credit cards. Out-of-town checks OK with ID.

Chuck's Supper Club on Silver Lake
American
37238 Valley Rd., Oconomowoc / 414-567-6911
(From I-94, Exit #282, N on Hwy. 67, W on Hwy. B)

This venerable supper club has been owned and operated since 1947 by the Chuck family. Patrons can enjoy beautiful sunsets over Silver Lake while enjoying juicy prime rib, shrimp supreme, parmesan shrimp, salmon steak, filet mignon, New York strip steaks, roast duckling, and chicken cordon bleu. This is a favorite destination for many diners on Friday night, for the fish and chicken fry—all you care to eat.

Moderate. Most dinners $11-19 (light dinners $7-10). Serving Sun. 3:30-9, weekdays 5-9:30, Fri. 4:30-10, Sat. 5-10. Closed Tues. except Jun., Jul., & Aug. Parking lot. Wheelchair accessible. Smoking & nonsmoking sections. Cocktail lounge/bar. Children's menu. Seniors discount (age 60+). Reservations recommended. Takeouts. Live music & dancing Fri. eves. Apr.-Oct. & Dec. Private parties (max. 380). MC, VI, AE. Out-of-town checks OK with ID.

Weissgerber's Golden Mast Inn
German
1270 Lacy's Lane, Okauchee / 414-567-7047

The Golden Mast Inn was founded in 1968, overlooking beautiful Okauchee Lake. There is a large fireplace in the dining room and, in summer, patrons can enjoy a large outdoor patio overlooking the lake. The menu here features many German specialties, including wiener schnitzel and roast duck, and also many American dishes. The prime rib is outstanding.

Expensive. Most dinners $15-19. Serving Sun. 11-3 (brunch) & 3-9, Mon.-Thurs. 5-10, Fri.-Sat. 5-11. Parking lot. Wheelchair accessible. Smoking & nonsmoking sections. Cocktail lounge/bar. Children's menu. Reservations recommended. Catering service. Live music Fri. eves. in summer. Private parties (max. 225). MC, VI, AE. Out-of-town checks OK with ID.

Michael's House of Prime
Supper club
W278 N2316 Hwy. 55, Pewaukee / 414-691-1450
(From I-94, Exit #290 N)

This supper club, founded in 1977, is known throughout the area for great prime rib, but there is also a full supper club menu featuring steaks, poultry, seafood, and veal dishes.

Expensive. Most dinners $15-18. Serving Sun.-Thurs. 5-10, Fri. 4:30-11 (until 10 in winter), Sat. 5-11 (until 10 in winter). Nearby public parking. Not wheelchair accessible. No policy on smoking. Cocktail lounge/bar. Children's menu. Reservations recommended. MC, VI. No checks.

Saz's & Pep's Depot
Supper club
319 Williams, Waukesha / 414-547-1722

This restaurant is related to the famous Saz's on State Street, and the barbequed ribs at the Depot are from the same award-winning recipe. The barbecued chicken is also out of this world, and the menu has a lot of other tempting selections, as well. Patrons here can dine in an 1881 train station, or eat in a dining car on the rails. For railroad buffs, this is the place to go in Waukesha County.

Inexpensive to moderate. Most dinners $8-16. Serving Sun. 10:30-3 (brunch) & 4-9, Mon.-Thurs. 11-10, Fri. & Sat. 11-11. Parking lot. Wheelchair accessible. Smoking & nonsmoking sections. Cocktail lounge/bar. Children's menu. Reservations not accepted. Local deliveries. Takeouts. Catering service. Live music Wed., Sat., & Sun eves. Private parties (max. 85). MC, VI, AE, Dis. Out-of-town checks OK with ID.

Weissgerber's Gasthaus
German
2720 N. Grandview Blvd., Waukesha / 414-544-4460
(From I-94, 1 blk S on Hwy. T)

This is old world dining in Waukesha, hosted by the famous Weissgerber family. Warm woodwork, a fieldstone fireplace, and colorful stained-glass windows provide a comfortable and intimate atmosphere. German and Continental favorites include pork shank, sauerbraten, beef rouladen, kasseler rippchen (roast pork loin served with red cabbage and mashed potatoes), wiener schnitzel and other veal dishes, and lamb shank. There are four sausage platters and a full list of American favorites—steaks, prime rib, calf's liver, catfish, chicken, and more. Very popular is the Friday night fish fry, with a choice of fried or steamed fish.

Expensive. Most dinners $16-18. Serving Sun. 4-9, Mon.-Fri. 11:30-2:30 & 5-10, Sat. 5-10. Parking lot. Wheelchair accessible. Smoking & nonsmoking sections. Cocktail lounge/bar. Children's menu. Reservations recommended (essential on Sat., but not accepted for Fri. fish fry). Takeouts for fish fry. Catering service. Private parties (max. 125). MC, VI, AE. Out-of-town checks OK with ID.

Wildflowers Restaurant
American
2810 Golf Rd., Waukesha / 414-547-0201
(From I-94, exit Hwy. T on Golf Rd.)

Here is a real taste of the country, just a stone's throw from Milwaukee. Wildflowers is located in the Country Inn Hotel, offering both hotel guests and others fine food and warm hospitality. Standard menu entrees include tenderloin with roasted garlic and shiitake mushrooms, chicken and shrimp pesto sauteed with mushrooms, tomatoes, and linguine, hunter's-style pork tenderloin sauteed with mushrooms, shallots, and brown mustard, and orange roughy sauteed with bananas, pineapple, and pecans. There is also a "chef's specialties" side of the menu that changes monthly. The menu we have lists veal Saltimbocca rolled with sage, prosciutto, and romano, marinated swordfish brochettes, king salmon poached in a court-bouillon, and vegetarian lasagne. There is also a selection of sandwiches and salads. Also in the hotel is Copper's Pub & Grill, serving 140 brands of beer, light dinners, and pizza.

Moderate. Most dinners $10-15. Serving Sun. 6:30 am-10 pm (brunch 9-1), Mon.-Thurs. 6:30-2 & 5-10, Fri. 6:30-2 & 4-10, Sat. 6:30-2 & 5-10. Parking lot. Wheelchair accessible. Smoking & nonsmoking sections. Cocktail lounge/bar. Children's menu. Children's birthday parties. Reservations recommended. Takeouts. Private parties (max. 550). MC, VI, AE, Dis, DC. Out-of-town checks cashed at front desk.

The Poplar Place
American
518 Poplar St., West Bend / 414-334-9292
(From Main St. go W on Poplar St., 1-1/2 blks)

The Poplar Place is located in a historic 125-year-old cream city brick building which once housed the deeds of Washington County. It later served as a private home and is now a charming restaurant. The atmosphere is relaxed and casual in any of the Poplar Place's three dining rooms, two of them upstairs, where you will also find a unique pub. The Poplar Place is known for its homemade soups, popovers, and desserts, but the broad-based menu includes steaks, fresh fish, shrimp stir-fry, chicken dishes, roast pork, and a variety of sandwiches. There are fish specials on Friday night, and a selection of light entrees.

Inexpensive. Most dinners $5-7. Serving lunch Mon.-Fri. 11-2, dinner Thur.-Sat. from 5:30. Closed Sun. Parking lot. Wheelchair accessible. Smoking & nonsmoking sections. Cocktail lounge/bar. Children's menu. Reservations recommended. Takeouts. Private parties (max. 40). MC, VI. Out-of-town checks OK with ID.

LAKE GENEVA & VICINITY
Including Williams Bay

The Grandview Restaurant & Lounge
The Geneva Inn
American / Continental
N2009 Hwy. 120, Lake Geneva / 414-248-5680 or 1-800-441-5881
(2-1/2 mi S of downtown Lake Geneva)

The Grandview, located in the 37-room Geneva Inn, was established in 1990 as a modern-day version of a traditional English inn. It is the only restaurant located on the south shore of Geneva Lake. There are grand sunsets on view from the dining room windows, and a full menu of steaks, seafood, and other specialties. The Grandview prides itself on its fresh fish, including salmon and swordfish, rack of lamb, and char-grilled steaks. Appetizers include escargot and mushroom strudel, and salads feature a Caesar salad and mixed lettuce with brie. For an elegant and secluded getaway in busy Lake Geneva, this is the place to go.

Expensive. Most dinners $16-20. Serving Sun. brunch 10:30-2:30, dinner 3-9. Other days, lunch 11:30-2:30, dinner 5-10 (10:30 on Fri.-Sat.). Valet parking. Private boat slips. Wheelchair accessible. Proper attire required. Smoking & nonsmoking sections. Cocktail lounge/bar. Children's menu. Reservations recommended. Live piano music daily during season, weekends only Nov.-Apr. Private parties (max. 80). All major credit cards. No checks.

Popeye's
American
811 Wrigley Dr., Lake Geneva / 414-248-4381
(In downtown Lake Geneva, across the street from
public beach and boat docks)

Popeye's is one of the most fun places to eat in the Lake Geneva area. It is a sprawling restaurant, seating more than 500, and it offers a great view of the lake. In good weather, you'll love the glass-enclosed deck area, which is most festive. From April through October, the cooks roast chicken, lamb, and pork on the outdoor spits, and patrons all year-round love the homemade pies and soups at Popeye's. The broccoli-cheese soup is especially recommended. This is one of my favorite summertime restaurants in southern Wisconsin.

Moderate. Most dinners $10-13. Serving Sun.-Thurs. 11:30-9, Fri.-Sat. 11:30-10. Small parking lot. (Public parking lot 2 blks.) Wheelchair accessible. Smoking & nonsmoking sections. Full bar. Children's menu. Reservations not accepted (but preferred seating for large groups). Takeouts on weekdays only. Catering service. Private parties (including DJ & dancing; max. 220). MC, VI, AE, Dis. No checks.

The Red Geranium
Continental / American
7194 Hwy. 50 East, Lake Geneva / 414-248-3637
(Intersection of Hwys. 12 & 50)

The Red Geranium, a converted farmhouse adorned with a variety of fireplaces, opened in 1985. The restaurant is decorated in red geranium wallpaper in the small individual dining rooms, perfect for intimate dining, while the Garden Room, stenciled in red geraniums and accented by a recently added grand piano, can accommodate up to 75 people for private parties, with access to the adjacent courtyard for additional outdoor activities. The menu features a variety of steak, seafood, and poultry selections, including daily lunch and dinner specials.

Moderate to expensive. Most dinners $13-18. Serving Sun. plated brunch 11-2, dinner 4-9. Mon.-Sat. lunch 11-2:30, dinner from 5 pm. Parking lot. Wheelchair accessible. Smoking & nonsmoking sections. Cocktail lounge/bar. Reservations recommended. Catering service. Piano music Fri. & Sat. evenings. Private parties (max. 75). MC, VI, AE, Dis. No checks.

Kirsch's Restaurant
Continental / French
Hwy. 50 West, Williams Bay / 414-245-5756
(On Hwy. 50, 3-1/2 mi W of the town of Lake Geneva)

Kirsch's, which shares a lovely old building with the French Country Inn, a B&B, is one of the most romantic spots in the Lake Geneva area. It is decorated in the French country style and is blessed with beautiful sunsets. Everything at Kirsch's is homemade, stresses manager Tracey Cole, including the ice cream, salad dressings, and soups. Certified Angus steaks and fresh fish are two of the specialties of this most pleasant restaurant.

Expensive. Most dinners $14-19. Serving dinner Mon.-Sat. 5-10 (5-9 in winter). Sun. brunch in summer 11:30-2:30, dinner 5-10. Parking lot. Wheelchair accessible. Cocktail lounge. Children's portions. Reservations strongly recommended. Private parties (max. 115). MC, VI, AE, DI. Out-of-town checks OK with ID.

BELOIT / JANESVILLE

Camboni's Butterfly Club
Supper club
Rte. 1, Hwy. X, Beloit / 608-362-8577
(From I-90 to I-43 N; exit 2/Hart Rd., right on Hart, left on Cty. Hwy. X)

Camboni's has been operating in Beloit since 1924, and has been under its present ownership since 1977. Ric Camboni serves up a full supper club menu of steaks, chicken, seafood, and pasta. Specialties include prime rib, and an all-you-can-eat fish fry on both Wednesdays and Fridays. The restaurant grounds are decorated with tulips in the spring, and there is outdoor dining on the deck from Memorial Day to Labor Day. For fine dining, Camboni's is a good bet for visitors and locals alike.

Inexpensive to moderate. Most dinners $9-15. Serving dinner Sun. noon-8, weekdays 5-9:30, Fri. 4:30-10, Sat. 5-10. Parking lot. Wheelchair accessible. Smoking & nonsmoking sections. Cocktail lounge/bar. Entertainment Fri. & Sat. eves. Children's menu. Reservations recommended. Private parties (max. 100). MC, VI, AE, Dis. No checks.

The Gun Club
Supper club
Rt. 1, Colley Rd., Beloit / 608-362-9900

The Gun Club has been a staple in Beloit for more than a half-century, but under its present ownership only since 1990. It is a casual supper club with an all-wood decor, country furnishings, and lots of antiques. It is known for its outstanding decorations during the holiday season. The menu here emphasizes steaks, prime rib, and lamb chops, although fish, seafood, and chicken dishes are also available. A piano player entertains on Friday and Saturday nights, playing jazz, blues, and big band tunes.

Moderate. Most dinners $9-15. Serving Sun. noon-8, weekdays 5-close, Fri. 4:30-close, Sat. 5-close. Parking lot. Wheelchair accessible. Smoking & nonsmoking sections. Cocktail lounge/bar. Children's menu. Reservations essential. Private parties (max. 40). MC, VI, DC. Out-of-town checks OK with ID.

Cafe Marsay
Continental / French
2002 E. Milwaukee St., Janesville / 608-752-2299
(On Cty. Hwy. A between I-90 Exits 171 & 176)

This European-style restaurant offers excellent food and an atmosphere enhanced by fine paintings and antiques. Specialties include seafood dishes, prime rib, and excellent steaks.

Moderate. Most dinners $9-15. Serving Sun. brunch 7 am-2 pm, Mon. 6:30 am-2 pm, Tue.-Sat. 6:30 am-9 pm. Parking lot. Wheelchair accessible. Smoking & nonsmoking sections. Cocktail lounge/bar. Children's portions. Reservations recommended. Local deliveries. Takeouts. Keyboard music Sat. nights. Private parties (max. 35). MC, VI, AE. Out-of-town checks OK with ID.

Campi's Prime Rib
Supper club
4323 Milton Ave. (Hwy. 26), Janesville / 608-785-0321

Campi's, recently remodeled, is *the* place to go in Janesville for prime rib. The dining room offers a very romantic view of Janesville.

Inexpensive to expensive. Most dinners $8-35. Serving weekdays 5-10, Fri. 4-10, Sat. 5-10, Sun. 4-9. Parking lot. Wheelchair accessible. No policy on smoking. Cocktail lounge. Children's menu. Reservations recommended. Private parties (max. 110). MC, VI, AE. Out-of-town checks OK with ID.

Cracker Barrel
American country style
2430 Fulton St., Janesville / 608-752-7750
(Exit I-90 at Exit #171)

Virtually no chain restaurants are included in this book, but the Janesville Cracker Barrel happens to be one of the better restaurants in the area. (Corporate headquarters are in Lebanon, Tennessee.) The Cracker Barrel decor is meant to evoke the image of a turn-of-the-century country store, with farm implements and other country artifacts spread about. There is also a gift shop in keeping with the country theme. The menu runs to items such as chicken and dumplings, steak and biscuits, pork chops, and fish. It is a good place to take the kids, and it won't break the family budget.

Inexpensive. Most dinners under $10. Serving Sun.-Thurs. 6 am-10 pm, Fri.-Sat. 6 am-11 pm. Parking lot. Wheelchair accessible. Smoking & nonsmoking sections. No alcohol. Children's menu. Reservations not accepted. MC, VI, AE, Dis. No checks.

EAST SHORE
Including Elkhart Lake, Kohler, Plymouth, Port Washington, Sheboygan, and Two Rivers

Siebkens Resort
American
284 S. Lake St., Elkhart Lake / 414-876-2600
(N on Hwy. 57 past Plymouth, left on Cty. J & right on Hwy. 67 to Elkhart Lake)

Since 1916, four generations of Siebkens have run this rustic lodge, situated on the beautiful shores of spring-fed Elkhart Lake. There is an antique and gift shop, and a sandwich shop and tavern open seven nights a week. Antique hanging lamps and brightly flowered curtains decorate the rambling porch where meals are served. The menu changes daily, and features fresh foods of the season, including many regional foods.

Moderate. Most dinners $10-16. Serving Sun. 9-11, 12-2, & 6-9. Thurs. 6-9. Fri. 12-2 & 6-9. Sat. 9-11, 12-2 & 6-9. Parking lot. Wheelchair accessible. Smoking & nonsmoking sections. Cocktail lounge/bar. Small children not encouraged. Reservations recommended. Takeouts. Occasional evening entertainment. No credit cards. Out-of-town checks OK with ID.

★ ★ ★

The Immigrant Restaurant
at the American Club
American / Regional cuisine
Highland Dr., Kohler / 414-457-8888
(From I-43, Exit #126 at Kohler)

Here is one of the most elegant restaurants in the state, located in a similarly elegant resort about three miles southwest of Sheboygan. The American Club, listed on the National Register of Historic Places, was founded in 1918. The resort includes 237 guest rooms, conference facilities, two 18-hole golf courses, a private spa, fitness and racquet clubs, a 500-acre wildlife preserve for outdoor activities, and five restaurants, of which the Immigrant is the most famous. American Club head chef Rhys Lewis and Immigrant Restaurant chef Mark Otto use the best of Wisconsin regional foods in creating dishes. Prominent on the menu are Wisconsin cheeses, fruits and vegetables of the season, Great Lakes fish, and Wisconsin farm meats. Here, you might find Wisconsin Heartland wild game ragout, fresh lake trout sauteed with crushed pecans and served with a brandy-butter sauce, or classic rack of lamb. The desserts at the Immigrant are legendary, including many made with fresh Wisconsin fruits, others, such as praline souffle, inspired creations of the chef. You will long remember a visit to the Immigrant. (Other restaurants at the American Club include the Horse 'n Plow, the Wisconsin Room, Cucina at the Shops, and the Blackwolf Run Clubhouse.)

Expensive. Most dinners $24-31. Serving dinner Tue.-Fri. 6-10, Sat. 6-11. Closed Sun. & Mon. (Sun. brunch 11-2 in the Wisconsin Room.) Underground parking. Wheelchair accessible. Smoking & nonsmoking sections. Cocktail lounge/bar. Small children not encouraged. Reservations recommended. Catering service (American Club Banquets & Catering Dept.). Pianist in the Winery Lounge Fri.-Sat. nights. Dancing Fri.-Sat. Private parties (max. 18 in Immigrant; otherwise call banquet mgr.). All major credit cards. Out-of-town checks OK with ID.

---

52 Stafford
Irish guest house
52 Stafford St., Plymouth / 414-893-0552
(In downtown Plymouth at the traffic lights)

This magnificent 1892 inn, on the National Register of Historic Places, has been beautifully restored by owner and operator Cary James "Rip" O'Dwanny. There are nineteen guest rooms, a fine period bar, and a dining room featuring tooled millwork, stained glass windows, and a tin ceiling. The menu is limited and changes often, but contains a variety of chicken, veal, steak, and seafood dishes.

A specialty of the house is Guinness brisket, a platter of thin-sliced beef brisket simmered in Guinness stout and served with Colcannon, an Irish concoction of potatoes, cabbage, milk, butter, parsley, and leeks.

Moderate. Most dinners $10-15. Serving Sun.-Thurs. 5-9, Fri.-Sat. 5-10. Parking lot. Not wheelchair accessible. Smoking & nonsmoking sections. Irish pub. Reservations recommended. Live Irish, folk, & jazz music weekend nights. Private parties (max. 80). All major credit cards. Out-of-town checks OK with ID.

Buchel's Colonial House
Continental
1000 S. Spring St. (Hwy. 32), Port Washington
414-375-1180 or 284-2212

Cuisine in the Continental style is the tradition at Buchel's. Chef Walter Buchel is the son of "Papa" Joseph Buchel, who was personal chef to Franz Joseph II, Prince of Liechtenstein, and an ardent disciple of the legendary Auguste Escoffier, "the king of cooks and the cook of kings." Papa Buchel's legacy is evident in the cuisine of this fine restaurant. Continental specialties include beef rouladen with spatzels, beef tenderloin Parisienne, veal Zurich, beef stroganoff, veal Saltimbocca, chicken Kiev, French pepper steak, and Hungarian goulash. There are also fresh seafood specialties. All soups, sauces, and desserts are homemade.

Moderate to expensive. Most dinners $10-20. Serving dinner daily 5-10, Sun. until 9. Closed Mon. Parking lot. Wheelchair accessible. Separate smoking & nonsmoking rooms. Cocktail lounge. Children's portions. Reservations recommended. Catering service. Private parties (max. 80). MC, VI. Out-of-town checks OK with ID.

Port Hotel Restaurant
Supper club
101 E. Main St., Port Washington / 414-284-9473

A two-pound porterhouse? Yes, the Port has long been known for both the quality and quantity of its steaks, as well as prime rib and fresh seafood. A local favorite since 1973.

Inexpensive to moderate. Most dinners $6-15. Serving Mon.-Thur.11:30-2 & 5-10, Fri. 11:30-2 & 5-11, Sat. 4:30-11, Sun. brunch 11-2, dinner 5-10. Parking lot. Dining area wheelchair accessible (rest rooms not accessible). Smoking & nonsmoking sections. Cocktail lounge. Children's menu. Reservations essential. Takeouts. Private parties (max. 75). All major credit cards. No checks.

City Streets Riverside
American
712 Riverfront Dr., Sheboygan / 414-457-9050
(From I-43, Hwy. 23 E to Sixth St., turn R to restaurant)

This fine restaurant is in a century-old building overlooking Sheboygan's historic
Fish Shanty Village. The atmosphere is casual, and there are some good fish
and seafood entrees here, including Maryland crab cakes, fresh water whitefish,
scallops with linguine, shrimp scampi, orange roughy, and Atlantic salmon.
For landlubbers there are steaks, prime rib, pork chops, barbequed Chinese ribs,
Peking-style duck, and other tempting entrees. City Streets also has a good selection of soups, salads, and light entrees.

Moderate. Most dinners $10-15. Serving Mon.-Thurs. 11-2 & 5-9, Fri. 11-2 & 5-
10, Sat. 5-10. Closed Sun. Parking lot. Wheelchair accessible. Smoking & nonsmoking sections. Cocktail lounge/bar. Children's menu. Special "early bird"
classic dinners. Reservations recommended. Takeouts. Catering service. Private
parties (max. 500). MC, VI, AE, DC, CB. Out-of-town checks OK with ID.

Rupp's Lodge
Supper club
925 N. Eighth St., Sheboygan / 414-459-8155

Rupp's has been a Sheboygan landmark since 1935, under present ownership
since 1979. It is a beautiful older restaurant with a back bar that dates to 1939.
A unique touch is the glassed-in kitchen where customers can watch their
own steaks being prepared. Specialties on the supper club menu include steaks
(all meat hand-cut on the premises), large barbequed ribs, baby beef liver, and
jumbo shrimp.

Moderate. Most dinners $8-15. Serving weekdays 11-10, Fri.-Sat. until 10:30.
Sun 10:30-9 (brunch 10:30-2). Wheelchair accessible. Smoking & nonsmoking
sections. Cocktail lounge. Children's portions. Special "early bird" prices. Reservations recommended. Takeouts. Catering service. Fri.-Sat. piano singalongs.
Private parties (max. 75). MC, VI, AE, Dis, DC. Out-of-town checks OK with ID.

Kurtz's Pub & Deli
American
1410 Washington St., Two Rivers / 414-793-1222
(On Hwy. 42 in downtown Two Rivers)

Charles Kurtz founded this establishment in 1904, serving sailing merchants who docked near the Two Rivers Marine Exchange. Nine decades and several moves later, the same family still owns and runs the pub and deli, now serving townspeople and tourists as well as sailors. The bar has a great selection of imported beers and crunchy snacks. The menu lists a broad selection of hot and cold sandwiches, salads, a soup of the day, and lots of desserts including sundaes. (The ice cream sundae, in fact, was invented right here in Two Rivers, in 1881, and Kurtz's pays proper respect to this history.) For those stopping here on the way to Door County, I especially recommend "Kurtz's Delight"—Door County cherries, homemade hot fudge, and whipped cream on two scoops of vanilla ice cream. What a way to start a vacation!

Inexpensive. All items under $5. Serving Mon.-Sat. 11-11. Closed Sun. Parking lot. Not wheelchair accessible. Cocktail lounge/bar. Reservations recommended. Takeouts. Private parties (max. 35). MC, VI, Dis.

The Water's Edge In The Lighthouse Inn
Supper club
1515 Memorial Dr., Two Rivers / 414-793-4524
(On Hwy. 42, at the lakeshore)

James Van Lanen, Jr., says it right out: "We have the best view of the lake in the world!" That's Lake Michigan, of course, and the view from this traditional supper club is indeed wonderful. The dining room is a scant twenty feet from the shore, and the big picture windows offer a fine view. The food is fine, too, centering on steaks, chicken, and an outstanding selection of fish and seafood, including lobster tail, Alaskan crab, Great Lakes whitefish, gulf shrimp, Idaho rainbow trout, ocean scallops, swordfish, orange roughy, and Las Vegas-style flounder (stuffed with fresh crab meat and baked). There are also nightly specials, a good selection of heart-smart entrees, a light dining menu, a large selection of desserts, and a Sunday brunch. You'll find everything you want at the Water's Edge.

Moderate. Most dinners $10-15. Serving Sun. 7:30 am-10 pm (in winter until 9). Sun. brunch 10-2. Mon.-Thurs. 6:30 am-10 pm (in winter until 9), Fri. & Sat. 6:30 am-10 pm. Parking lot. Wheelchair accessible. Smoking & nonsmoking sections. Cocktail lounge/bar. Children's portions. Reservations recommended. Local deliveries. Takeouts. Catering service. Live music (soft rock & country) Fri. & Sat. eves. Private parties (max. 400). MC, VI, AE. No checks.

FOX RIVER VALLEY
Including Appleton, Fond du Lac, Green Bay, and Oshkosh

Le Bon Appetit
Continental / French
3301 W. Prospect Ave., Appleton / 414-738-0012
(From Hwy. 41, exit BB/Prospect Ave., go E 1/8th mi)

This is an upscale restaurant with a French country atmosphere. From the many windows throughout the restaurant, diners can look out onto the beautifully land-scaped grounds. There is also a French-style courtyard complete with a fountain, tables, and chairs. Bastille Day (July 14) calls for a special celebration, with cooking in the courtyard. The cuisine at Le Bon Appetit centers on fresh seafood, innovative veal dishes, and French desserts.

Moderate to Expensive. Most dinners $13-19. Serving Mon.-Fri. lunch 11-2, dinner 5-9. Sat. until 10. Closed Sun. Off-street parking. Wheelchair accessible. Smoking & nonsmoking sections. Cocktail lounge. Children's portions. Reservations recommended. Takeouts. Private parties (max. 125). MC, VI, AE. Out-of-town checks OK with ID.

The Colony
Supper club
15 W. Division St., Fond du Lac / 414-921-2200
(At Division & Main Sts. in downtown Fond du Lac)

Here is an old-fashioned supper club with a traditional menu and traditional values. David Ransom has owned and operated the Colony since 1969, and has become well-known for his beer-batter fish, prime rib, express lunch buffet, and free birthday dinners. The restaurant features a 1,600-light starlight lounge for dancing (Wednesday, Friday, and Saturday nights) with a DJ spinning music from the 1940s, 1950s, and 1960s. The show is broadcast on a local AM station on Saturday nights.

Inexpensive. Most dinners $6-11. Serving Mon.-Fri. 11-2 & 4:30-closing. Sat. 4:30-closing. Closed Sun. Parking lot. Wheelchair accessible. Smoking & non-smoking sections. Cocktail lounge/bar. Children's menu. Children's birthday parties. Reservations recommended. Takeouts. Catering service. Private parties (max. 350). MC, VI, AE, Dis, DC, CB. No checks.

Schreiner's
American
168 N. Pioneer Rd., Fond du Lac / 414-922-0590
(Intersection of Hwys. 41 & 23)

Schreiner's is a cheerful, well-lit, and sprawling family restaurant with a long-standing and well-deserved reputation for good food and moderate prices. Paul Cunningham worked for the Schreiner family for 23 years before buying the restaurant in 1992, and he is dedicated to continuing the tradition that has been pleasing patrons since 1938. Schreiner's is best known for its New England-style clam chowder, baked goods (made on the premises), and scratch-prepared soups, gravies, and entrees. The regular menu is broad, and daily specials include stewed chicken and dumplings (Tues.), ham loaf (Mon.), roast loin of pork (Wed.), and butter-baked chicken (Sun.). For hearty meals and good value, Schreiner's is unbeatable in the Fond du Lac area.

Inexpensive. Most dinners $5-7. Serving daily 6:30 am-9 pm (until 10 mid-Jul. to mid-Aug.). Parking lot. Wheelchair accessible. Smoking & nonsmoking sections. Full bar. Children's menu. Mini-menu (lighter portions and smaller prices) 11 am-2:30 pm. weekdays only. Takeouts. MC, VI, AE, Dis. Out-of-town checks OK with ID.

La Bonne Femme
Continental / French
123 S. Washington, Green Bay / 414-432-2897

This is the most romantic dining spot in Green Bay, as well as the only restaurant in town serving exclusively French cuisine. The atmosphere is country-French, quite intimate, the place to go with a special date or to celebrate a wedding anniversary. The menu changes regularly, enabling the restaurant to take advantage of fresh foods of the season and momentary inspiration of the chef, and is presented verbally by the servers. There is live classical music presented on Thursdays and on some weekend nights.

Moderate to expensive. Most dinners $13-18. Serving Tues.-Fri. lunch 11:30-1:30, dinner 5-9. Sat. dinner only, 5-9. Closed Sun.-Mon. Public parking lot nearby. Easy curb parking. Dining room wheelchair accessible (rest rooms not accessible). Children welcomed. Children's portions. Full bar. Reservations recommended. Private parties. MC, VI, AE. Out-of-town checks OK with ID.

Zimmani's
Italian / Nouveau
333 Main St., Green Bay / 414-436-2340
(Located downtown in the Regency Center, 2 blks E of the Fox River)

This excellent restaurant, with a cool, art-deco, deli atmosphere, is best known for its outstanding pasta dishes. Zimmani's makes good use of the newer forms of pasta, including mushroom and whole-wheat pasta, and uses them with some very creative sauces. There are also some non-Italian dishes, including blackened catfish and some Asian dishes. The desserts here are excellent, as well, including some of the best cheesecake in the Fox River Valley.

Moderate to expensive. Most dinners $11-17. Serving Mon.-Thurs. 11-9, Fri.-Sat. 11-10. Dessert & coffee until midnight. Closed Sun. Curb parking. Wheelchair accessible. Smoking & nonsmoking sections. Cocktail lounge/bar. Small children not encouraged. Reservations recommended. Local lunch deliveries. Takeouts. Catering service. MC, VI, AE, Dis, DC. Out-of-town checks OK with ID.

Butch's Anchor Inn
Supper club / Seafood
225 W. 20th St., Oshkosh / 414-236-5360
(From Hwy. 41, Exit #44 toward Oshkosh, right at 2d traffic light,
4 blks past Wittman Airport Terminal)

Butch's Anchor Inn is a supper club *extraordinaire*. The restaurant features an antique nautical decor with an 800-gallon shark tank and five other aquariums. There are "huts" for private dining, seating two to eight people, and some of the best food to ever grace a Wisconsin supper club, prepared under the supervision of owner/chef John L. Arps. Permanent entrees on the menu include prime rib, steaks, veal Oscar, walleyed pike, lobster tail, shrimp, scallops, perch, haddock, bouillabaisse, and chicken cordon bleu. There are also nightly specials such as chateaubriand, seafood Alfredo, fresh fish, pepper-bacon wrapped scallops, barbecued ribs, and veal and chicken dishes. All the breads, soups, sauces, and pastries are homemade. The menu has a special light-dining section, and the kitchen will be happy to prepare a meal to be low in fat and cholesterol, on request.

Moderate to expensive. Most dinners $10-18. Serving Sun. 10-10 (brunch 10-2:30), Mon.-Thurs. 11-10, Fri.-Sat. 11-11. Parking lot. Wheelchair accessible. Smoking and nonsmoking sections. Cocktail lounge/bar. Children's menu. Special menu for "early birds" and seniors (age 59+) Sun.-Thurs. 4-6 pm. Reservations recommended. Takeouts. Catering service. Private parties (max. 225). MC, VI, AE, Dis. Out-of-town checks OK with ID.

The Granary
American
50 W. Sixth Ave., Oshkosh / 414-233-3929
(From Hwy. 41, exit Ninth Ave. E to Oregon St., N 2 blks to Sixth St., E
2 blks to restaurant)

The Granary, established in 1984, is the result of a massive renovation project of an 1883 stone flour mill. When first entering the restaurant, you can see up into the towering chutes that once held trainloads of wheat and barley. A grand staircase takes you to the balcony dining room. A two-tiered barroom features a gigantic laddered back bar. Specialties on the menu include naturally aged and hand-cut prime rib and steaks, fresh seafood, veal, chicken teriyaki, steak teriyaki, steamed vegetables, tenderloin Oscar, and seafood dishes including Alaskan king crab, swordfish, and fresh sea scallops. At lunch, there is a wide variety of platters, salads, and sandwiches available.

Moderate. Most dinners $11-16. Serving Sun. 5-10 (until 9 in winter), Mon.-Thurs. 11-2 & 5-10, Fri. 11-2 & 5-11, Sat. 5-11. Parking lot. Wheelchair accessible. Smoking & nonsmoking sections. Cocktail lounge/bar. A few children's items. Reservations recommended. Takeouts. Catering service. Private parties (max. 115). MC, VI, AE, Dis, DC.

The Italian Underground
Italian / Pizza
225 W. 20th St., Oshkosh / 414-236-5373
(Located under Butch's Anchor Inn; see above)

This quaint little trattoria has wonderful pizza and inexpensive Italian entrees for casual dining. The bricks in the brick-and-stone wall came from a building destroyed in the Great Chicago Fire of 1871. In addition to the traditional pizzas, the Underground offers duck sausage, Thai chicken, shrimp pesto, goat cheese, and barbecued chicken pizzas. There are also six pasta dishes, salads and side orders, soups, steaks, and sandwiches.

Inexpensive. Most dinners $7-10. Serving Mon.-Thurs. 5-10, Fri. & Sat. 5-11. Parking lot. Not wheelchair accessible. Smoking & nonsmoking sections. Cocktail lounge/bar. Children's menu. Takeouts. Catering service. Private parties (max. 60). MC, VI, AE, Dis. Out-of-town checks OK with ID.

Marco's Italian Gardens
Restaurant & lounge
2605 Jackson Dr., Oshkosh / 414-236-5376

Romantic dining in elegant surroundings best describes Marco's, a favorite in the Fox River Valley since 1980. Specialties of the house include fettucine "All Marco" forno style (including meatballs, Italian sausage, mushrooms, tomato sauce, and cheese), veal with lobster Alfredo, spiedini, and cioppino (crab, lobster tail, clam, shrimp, and red snapper, sauteed with shallots, mushrooms, and tomatoes). Mostly Italian, of course, the menu also includes American and Greek dishes including steaks, seafood, and lamb.

Inexpensive to moderate. Most dinners $7-14. Serving weekdays 11-10, Fri.-Sat. 11-11, Sun. 9-9. Parking lot. Wheelchair accessible. Smoking & nonsmoking sections. Cocktail lounge. Children's portions. Seniors discount (55). Reservations recommended. Takeouts. Private parties (max. 100). MC, VI, AE, Dis, DC. Out-of-town checks OK with ID.

DOOR COUNTY
Including Baileys Harbor, Ellison Bay, Fish Creek, Sister Bay, and Sturgeon Bay

Gordon Lodge
International cuisine
1420 Pine Dr., Baileys Harbor / 414-839-2331
(Take Co. Hwy. Q from Baileys Harbor or Ephraim, or south
from Sister Bay on Hwy. 57 to Co. Hwy. Q, then left)

The Gordon Lodge is a cherished Door County institution, in the family since its founding in 1928. Located on "the quiet side" of Door County, the restaurant offers fine international dining in a casual atmosphere. Come prepared to view some beautiful sunsets from this location on Lake Michigan and North Bay. Specialties of the house include prime rib, green chicken, steak au poivire, Caesar salad, rack of lamb, filet mignon, and veal chops. There is dancing to live music in the lounge during the season.

Moderate to expensive. Most dinners $13-24. Serving breakfast daily 7:30-10. Lunch daily 11:30-2:30. Dinner nightly 6-9 (Sat. until 9:30). Parking lot. Restrooms not wheelchair accessible. Smoking & nonsmoking sections. Cocktail lounge/bar. Children's items available. Reservations recommended. MC, VI, AE. No checks.

The Viking Restaurant
American cafe
12029 Hwy. 42, Ellison Bay / 414-854-2998
(In downtown Ellison Bay)

Here is another Door Country institution, serving hungry visitors since 1940. The Viking is best known for its outdoor fish boil, which is served daily from mid-May through October. In addition, there is a full supper club menu featuring chicken, steaks, pork, fish, seafood, chili, and specialties such as whitefish chowder. And, of course, you can count on Door County cherry pie for dessert. The Viking is a great place for both adults and children.

Inexpensive to moderate. Most dinners $9-12. Serving daily, 6 am-9 pm during season. In winter, 6 am-3 pm Sun.-Thurs., 6 am-8 pm Fri.-Sat. Parking lot. Wheelchair accessible. Smoking & nonsmoking sections. Beer & wine served. Children's portions. Children's birthday parties arranged. Reservations not accepted. Local deliveries. Takeouts. Catering service. Private parties (max. 100). MC, VI, AE, Dis. Out-of-town checks OK with ID.

Voight's
Supper club
12010 Hwy. 42, Ellison Bay / 414-854-2250
(In downtown Ellison Bay)

Voight's was founded in the 1930s, and has been owned and run by Randall Daubner since 1988. It is a well-known and well-respected Door County restaurant, known for its prime rib, barbequed ribs, roast duck, and fresh whitefish, perch, and walleye. Many visitors and locals alike go to Voight's for their famous seafood casserole or whitefish au gratin.

Inexpensive to expensive. Most dinners $8-22. Serving dinner nightly from 5 pm. Sunday brunch 10-2. Parking lot. Wheelchair accessible. Separate smoking & nonsmoking dining rooms. Cocktail lounge/bar. Children's menu. Reservations accepted. Takeouts. Catering service. Private parties (max. 120). MC, VI, AE, Dis, DC, CB. Out-of-town checks OK with ID.

The Wagon Trail Resort
Grandma's Restaurant & Bakery
Swedish
1041 Hwy. ZZ, Ellison Bay / 414-854-2385
(5 mi NE of Sister Bay on Lake Michigan side, on Rowleys Bay)

This is the "Home of Grandma's Pecan Roll," owned and operated by a Door County Swedish family since 1970. Grandma's bakery is the crown of the restaurant, and the famous pecan roll is the crown jewel. Some days, Grandma sells more than 1,500 pecan rolls! Breakfast is the big meal at the restaurant, especially the Swedish Breakfast Brunch, which includes various sweet bakery items, fresh local fruit with whipped cream, bacon, sausage, potato pancakes, eggs, and more. The lunch menu offers a variety of sandwiches and burgers. There are nightly dinner buffet specials, including the Swedish smorgasbord on Thursday and Saturday nights, the German buffet on Wednesday, and the country/seafood buffet on Friday. Grandma also hosts traditional Door County fish boils, and makes homemade soups and chili, old fashioned bread pudding, Swedish skorpa, and, of course, Door County cherry pie. Grandma is one busy lady! The restaurant, long a favorite of family travelers, overlooks beautiful Rowleys Bay.

Moderate: Most dinners $12-15. Serving daily 8 am-8 pm. Sun. brunch 8-2. Parking lot. Wheelchair accessible. Totally nonsmoking. No alcohol. Children's menu. Reservations not necessary, except for large groups. Catering service. Private parties (max. 325). MC, VI, AE, Dis. Out-of-town checks OK with ID.

The Cookery
American cafe
Hwy. 42, Fish Creek / 414-868-3634
(In downtown Fish Creek, across from the public beach)

Dick and Carol Skare opened the Cookery in 1977, and have since expanded it to seat 85 patrons and added a gift and takeout food shop, the Pantry. Hearty breakfasts are a staple at the Cookery. Blueberry or cherry buttermilk pancakes are a most popular item, but many people come for the baked goods—home-baked cinnamon and caramel rolls, pumpkin bread, and fruit danish. Lunch features a wide array of sandwiches and burgers, in addition to Carol's famous whitefish chowder, fresh salads, and open-face sandwiches. Dinner specialties include stir-fries, broiled whitefish with mustard dill, lake perch, country smoked pork chops, and nightly specials including Saturday prime rib, Sunday baked chicken, Monday old-fashioned meat loaf, and Friday?—you guessed it—deep-fried lake perch. At the Cookery you can also get a real root beer float, made with genuine Baumeister root beer from Kewaunee. The Cookery is a cheerful place with good food—just right for families with children.

Inexpensive to moderate. Most dinners $7-11. Serving daily 7 am-9 pm in season. Breakfast until noon. Dinner from 4 pm. Parking lot. Wheelchair accessible. Totally nonsmoking. Beer & wine served. Children's menu. Reservations recommended. MC, VI. Out-of-town checks OK with ID.

Greenwood
Supper club
N9087 Cty. Hwy. A, Fish Creek / 414-839-2451
(At the intersection of Cty. Hwys. A & F, 2 mi E of Fish Creek)

Greenwood has been a tradition in beautiful Door County since 1929. Specialties here include fresh local fish, including lake perch and whitefish, prime rib, and nightly specials. The atmosphere is decidedly casual.

Moderate. Most dinners $9-16. Serving dinner daily 5-10, June through October. Serving Fri.-Sat.-Sun. only November through May. Parking lot. Wheelchair accessible. Smoking & nonsmoking sections. Cocktail lounge/bar. Children's menu. Reservations not accepted. Takeouts. Private parties (45 max). No credit cards. Out-of-town checks OK with ID.

★ ★ ★
The White Gull Inn
Regional cuisine
4225 Main St., Fish Creek / 414-868-3517
(Turn W at the only stop sign in Fish Creek. Go to the water's edge)

The White Gull is the epitome of Door County itself. This famous inn has been serving visitors and locals since 1897. It was built across Green Bay, in Marinette, but was dragged 18 miles across the frozen bay sometime around the turn of the century. The White Gull is doubtless the most famous inn in Door County, featured nationally in scores of magazine and newspaper articles (including the *New York Times*) and in many books. Such a charming and historic inn deserves fine and hearty food, and owners Jan and Andy Coulson have seen that the kitchen provides just that. The fish boil here is justly famous, long presided over by Russ Ostrand, who doubles as a concertina player after he cooks up the fish. After watching the spectacular fish boil in the courtyard, guests move into the rustic dining room, there to enjoy the dining experience by candlelight. There is a full menu in addition to the fish boil. The White Gull can pride itself on its hearty breakfasts (including homemade coffee cake and cherry-stuffed French toast), daily luncheon specials, and elegant evening meals. Dennis Getto, restaurant critic of the *Milwaukee Journal*, declared this as one of the 25 best restaurants in Wisconsin. And, taking into account the entire dining experience, we are certainly inclined to agree. The White Gull even has its own cookbook, which you may pick up on your way out. (Have a spectacular fish boil in your own backyard!)

Moderate to expensive. Most dinners $13-19. Serving daily breakfast 7:30-noon, lunch noon-2:30, dinner 5:30-8, year-round. Parking lot. Wheelchair accessible. Totally nonsmoking. Beer & wine served. Children's menu. Dinner reservations recommended. Reservations not accepted for breakfast or lunch. Catering service. A classical guitar player entertains on Mon., Tues. & Thurs. in summer, on Fri. in winter. All major credit cards. Out-of-town checks OK with ID.

★ ★ ★

Al Johnson's Swedish Restaurant
Scandinavian-American
700-710 Bay Shore Dr., Sister Bay / 414-854-2626
(Downtown Sister Bay, on Hwy. 42)

Anyone who has ever been to Door County, even once, remembers Al Johnson's. It's the restaurant with the goats on the roof! Al started the restaurant in 1949, but it has grown considerably since then. In 1973, Al and Ingert Johnson purchased several log structures on a trip to Scandinavia and used them to build a new facade around the old restaurant. The next year they decided to sod the roof—and then added the goats to keep the sod trimmed. All of this has not detracted from the quality of food, which is among the very best in Door County. The menu contains many Scandinavian items, including Swedish pancakes, fruit soup, limpa (a sweet, light rye bread seasoned with orange peel and anise), lingonberry spread, and—in my opinion—the world's best Swedish meatballs. Reservations are not accepted, and in summer the wait for a table might seem awfully long, but do not leave Door County without at least one visit to Al Johnson's.

Moderate. Most dinners $10-16. Serving daily 6 am-9 pm year-round. Parking lot. Wheelchair accessible. Smoking & nonsmoking sections. No alcohol served. Children's menu. Reservations not accepted. Catering service (off-season only). MC, VI, AE, Dis. Out-of-town checks OK with ID.

Hotel du Nord
French / Northern Italian / Seafood
11000 Bay Shore Dr., Sister Bay / 414-854-4221

The Hotel du Nord, overlooking beautiful Green Bay (the bay, i.e., not the city), dates well back to the nineteenth century. Located a mile north of the famous Al Johnson's Swedish Restaurant, the Hotel du Nord has achieved a certain fame of its own, with dishes such as Salmon Alexander (sauteed and finished with lingonberries and dill sauce) and lamb seasoned with rosemary and garlic, all served in a very attractive dining room.

Expensive. Most dinners $15-27. Serving Sun. 9:30-2 & 5-10, weekdays 5-10, Fri.-Sat. 4:30-10. Off-street parking. Wheelchair accessible. Smoking & non-smoking sections. Cocktail lounge. Children's portions. Private parties. MC, VI, AE, Dis. Out-of-town checks OK with ID.

Glidden Lodge
American
4670 Glidden Dr., Sturgeon Bay / 414-743-4944
(On the shore, across Whitefish Bay from Whitefish Dunes State Park)

Here is one of the most romantic dining spots in all of Wisconsin. From a windowside table, you are a mere thirty feet from the Lake Michigan water's edge, looking between the trunks of cedar, birch, and pine trees. The interior of the dining room is dominated by stonework and pine woodwork, accented by forest green table linen. This is a dining spot to make you forget that pressures of job and city life ever existed. And, of course, you can stay in one of the lodge's suites and use all the resort amenities—sand beach, tennis courts, charter fishing boat, etc. The Glidden menu is limited but the cuisine is excellent. Specialties include fettuccini Alfredo, stuffed pork chops, barbecued ribs, and three chicken entrees. There are also three steaks and four fish and seafood entrees, including fresh Door County whitefish and walleye pike. Visitors accustomed to zipping past this area on the way to the upper peninsula are missing a good bet by not stopping at the Glidden Lodge. It's one of our favorite places in Door County.

Inexpensive to moderate. Most dinners $9-15. Serving Memorial Day through October. Tue-Thur. 8-1 & 6-9, Fri. & Sat. 8-1 & 5:30-10, Mon. 8-1. (Closed for dinner on Mon.) Parking lot. Wheelchair accessible. Totally nonsmoking. Full bar. Children's menu. Children's birthday parties. Private parties (max. 100). Catering service. Reservations recommended. MC, VI. Out-of-town checks OK with ID.

★ ★ ★
The Inn at Cedar Crossing
American / Country classic
336 Louisiana St., Sturgeon Bay / 414-743-4249
(Follow Business 42/57 to downtown Sturgeon Bay)

The Inn is located in an 1884 commercial building, which has served in a number of capacities over the years. Starting in 1985, the owners carried out an extensive restoration of the property, turning it into an elegant inn and restaurant, which opened to the public in 1986. The atmosphere is Victorian romantic, with fireplaces in all dining rooms. Innkeeper Terry Wulf is proud of her restaurant's dedication to scratch home cooking and distinctive regional cuisine. Many of the foods served are grown right in Door County. Appetizers include cheese-stuffed mushroom caps, fresh escargots, and Cedar Street Strudel, flaky phyllo dough wrapped around a blend of snow crab, goat cheese, spinach, tomato, and basil. Entrees include shrimp Athena (with fresh tomato herb sauce, topped with feta cheese), shrimp Alfredo, capered whitefish, and fresh fish of the day. There are three pasta selections, and some tempting poultry and game dishes, including Wisconsin duckling, pheasant sausage linguine, and Sicilian chicken ravioli. There are also several steaks and lamb from which to choose, and a roast pork loin with pungent cherry chutney. But do save room for dessert. All are home-made from scratch, right in the Inn's kitchen, using only fresh ingredients. Deep-dish cherry pie is a special specialty! This is one of the finest restaurants in Door County, and in all of Wisconsin.

Moderate to expensive. Most dinners $12-25. Serving Sun.-Thurs. 7 am-9 pm, Fri.-Sat. until 9:30. Sun. brunch 7-2 in winter, 7-2:30 in summer and fall. Parking lot. Wheelchair accessible. Smoking & nonsmoking sections. Cocktail lounge. Children's portions. Takeouts. Catering service. Live music Sat. night—classical & folk guitar, flamenco & classical. Private parties during winter (max. 21). MC, VI, Dis. Out-of-town checks OK with ID.

WISCONSIN DELLS / LAKE DELTON

Michael's Fireside In the Chula Vista Resort
Traditional steakhouse
River Road, Wisconsin Dells / 608-254-8366
(From I-90/94, Exit #87 to Hwy. 13 E into Wisconsin Dells, at 4th
stoplight N 3 mi on River Rd.)

In a romantic setting overlooking the Wisconsin River, Michael's offers great steaks, seafoods, and fancy poultry dishes. The restaurant has been under present ownership since 1951.

Moderate to expensive. Most dinners $12-38. Serving daily breakfast 7:30-11, lunch noon-3, dinner 5-10. Parking lot. Wheelchair accessible. No policy on smoking. Cocktail lounge/bar. Children's menu. Reservations recommended. Catering service. Dancing in the summer months. Private parties (max. 220). All major credit cards. No checks.

The Cheese Factory
International / Vegetarian
521 Wisconsin Dells Parkway, Wisconsin Dells / 608-253-6065
(From I-90/94, Exit #92, 1 mi N on Hwy. 12,
across from Greyhound track)

Here, in the land of steaks, fried shrimp, and barbecued ribs, is an outstanding restaurant specializing in international vegetarian cuisine. The Cheese Factory, under Master Chef Sage Louise, has searched around the world to bring interesting, delicious, and healthful foods to Dells visitors. Specialties such as exotic Peking Oriental, Bombay curry, incredible calzones, rich burgundy stroganoffs, blackened Cajun skewers, elegant fritters and tempura, homemade pastas, soups, salads, pizza, pita pockets, burritos, and more. There are also heavenly desserts, designer coffees, and live entertainment on weekends. For a complete break from the traditional supper club fare, the Cheese Factory is the ticket.

Inexpensive. Most dinners $6-9. Serving daily 11-9. Sun. brunch 10:30-2. Parking lot. Wheelchair accessible. Totally nonsmoking. No alcohol. Children's menu. Children's birthday parties. Seniors discount (age 65+). Reservations recommended. Takeouts. Catering service. Live entertainment Fri. & Sat. eves. Dancing Sat. eve. Private parties (max. 16). MC, VI, AE. Out-of-town checks OK with ID.

★ ★ ★
Wally's House of Embers
Supper club
935 Wisconsin Dells Parkway, Wisconsin Dells / 608-253-6411
(On Hwy.12, in downtown Wisconsin Dells)

In the Wisconsin Dells, amid the waterslides, miniature golf courses, and souvenir shops, are a couple of really good restaurants—and Wally's House of Embers is certainly one of them. Despite its size, the restaurant maintains a sense of intimacy by the effective use of lighting, room and curtain dividers, and table placement. There is antique furniture, Tiffany-style lamps, and several gas fireplaces. This restaurant is famous for its barbequed ribs, smoked in a specially designed smokehouse. The menu also features Austrian veal, Shrimp Fettuccini Louise, fresh salmon, and prime rib. For that very special evening out, Wally's offers the Omar Sharif Room, intimate dining for two. There is also the Valentino Room (intimate dining for four to eight people) and Barbara's Veranda, a new and spacious tropical atrium with a private bar. I think that Wally's House of Embers is an outstanding choice in the Wisconsin Dells area, one of the best restaurants in Wisconsin.

Moderate to expensive. Most dinners $10-25. Serving dinner 4:30-11 daily. Sun. buffet brunch 9-1. Closed month of March. Parking lot. Wheelchair accessible. Smoking and nonsmoking sections. Cocktail lounge/bar. Children's menu. Special "early bird" prices until 6:30. Reservations recommended. Live piano music on weekends. Private parties (max. 200). MC, VI, AE. Out-of-town checks OK with ID.

Fischer's Supper Club
Supper club
441 Wisconsin Dells Parkway South, Lake Delton / 608-253-7531

Fischer's has been a Lake Delton institution since 1948, and has always been owned by the same family, now in the third generation of ownership and management. It is certainly one of the premier restaurants in the Wisconsin Dells/Lake Delton area. Fischer's is best known for its fresh seafood, choice steaks (cut in house), succulent barbequed spare ribs, lamb, veal, and pasta specialties.

Inexpensive to moderate. Most dinners $7-17. Serving Sun.-Thurs. 4-10:30, Fri.-Sat. 4-11. Close one-half hour earlier in off-season (after Labor Day & before Memorial Day). Parking lot. Wheelchair accessible. Smoking & nonsmoking sections. Full bar. Children's menu. Reservations recommended. Catering service. Private parties (max. 300). MC, VI. In-state checks only with ID.

Jimmy's Del-Bar
Supper club
800 Wisconsin Dells Parkway South, Lake Delton / 608-253-1861
(2-1/2 mi S of Wisconsin Dells on Hwy. 12)

Established in 1943, this is one of the best, and best-known, supper clubs in the popular Wisconsin Dells area. The building, designed by a protege of Frank Lloyd Wright, features woodburning fireplaces and stained glass windows. Original watercolors line the walls. Jimmy's has a full menu of supper club traditional favorites, but is perhaps best known for its USDA prime-grade aged steaks, grilled fresh fish and shellfish, and pasta dishes.

Moderate to expensive. Most dinners $10-20. Serving dinner daily 4:30-10. (Closed Sun. & Mon. Nov. to Apr.) Parking lot. Wheelchair accessible. Smoking & nonsmoking sections. Cocktail lounge/bar. Children's menu. Reservations recommended. Takeouts. Live piano music daily during summer, Fri. & Sat. in winter. Private parties (max. 110). All major credit cards. No checks.

CENTRAL WISCONSIN
Including Friendship, Green Lake, Mosinee, Nekoosa, Plover, Stevens Point, Waupun, and Wisconsin Rapids

Carlson's Rustic Ridge
Supper club
2230 Town Rd., Friendship / 608-339-6300
(25 mi N of Wisconsin Dells)

Carlson's, overlooking Castle Rock Lake (one of Wisconsin's ten largest lakes) is known for its seafood Newburg, beef stroganoff, and prime rib. Visitors to this resort and fishing area can always count on quality food and fair prices at Carlson's. And late diners will appreciate Carlson's extended summer hours.

Moderate. Most dinners $9-15. Serving (summer hours) Sun. 10-10 (brunch 10-2). Weekdays 4-10. Fri.-Sat. 4-11. Easy parking. Wheelchair accessible. No policy on smoking. Cocktail lounge/bar. Children's menu. Reservations recommended. Takeouts. Catering service. MC, VI. Out-of-town checks OK with ID.

Alfred's
Supper club
506 Hill St., Green Lake / 414-294-3631
(In the heart of downtown Green Lake)

Alfred's has a luxurious Victorian decor, but don't let that fool you. It's a casual, relaxed, and friendly place with very good food. The specialties here are hand-cut steaks, homemade soups, breads, and desserts, and a large salad bar. There are also Italian specialties.

Moderate to expensive. Most dinners $8-20. Serving daily 5-10 pm. Easy curb parking nearby. Wheelchair accessible. Smoking & nonsmoking sections. Cocktail lounge/bar. Children's menu. Takeouts. Private parties (max. 24). MC, VI. Out-of-town checks OK with ID.

Carvers on the Lake
Continental / New American
N5529 Cty. A, Green Lake / 414-294-6931

Carvers is a restaurant and guest house, located in a 1925 lakeside mansion that once served as a grand private home of the Carver family, then became an elegant inn during the Great Depression. Famous guests such as Spencer Tracy and Richard Widmark have stayed here, and now the new owners, Michael and Mary Marks, are restoring guest rooms that have not been used in many years. In the restaurant, they maintain Mrs. Carver's philosophy of "serving well prepared food in an atmosphere worthy of such fine food." Specialties of the house include fettucine parmigiana, breast of duck with wild rice pancakes, shrimp etouffe, and Chicken Four Seasons (breast of chicken sauteed wth lobster, mushrooms, and shallots in a light Marsala cream sauce). Situated on the east side of the lake, Carvers offers spectacular sunset views from the Great Room bar, porch, or patio, a cheering fireplace in the Great Room, and a private pier for those who prefer to arrive by boat.

Expensive. Most dinners $17-19. Serving dinner Tues.-Sun. from 5 pm. Closed Mon. Closed Tues. in winter. Parking lot. Not wheelchair accessible. Nonsmoking dining room. Smoking allowed in cocktail lounge. Children accommodated. Reservations recommended. Piano music Sat. evenings. Private parties (max. 50). MC, VI. Out-of-town checks OK with ID.

★ ★ ★
The Grey Rock Mansion
Heidel House Resort
Continental / American
643 Illinois Ave., Green Lake / 414-294-3344

The Grey Rock Mansion has long been known as one of the finest restaurants in Wisconsin. Located in the Heidel House Resort and Conference Center, on beautiful Green Lake, the Grey Rock serves distinguished regional dishes in an elegant setting, replete with fireplaces and beautiful views. The building itself dates back to 1890, the restaurant to 1943. Specialties include Walleye Nouvelle, Salmon en Papillote, and succulent prime rib. The staff's motto is "Yes we can!", says general manager Margaret York—and, judging by our previous visits, we believe it fully.

Moderate. Most dinners $13-18. Serving weekdays breakfast 6:00-11, lunch 11:30-2, dinner 5-10. Fri.-Sat. dinner until 11. Sun. brunch 8-2, dinner 5-10. Parking lot. Wheelchair accessible. Smoking & nonsmoking sections. Cocktail lounge. Children welcome. Reservations recommended. Piano music & dancing Fri.-Sat. nights. Private parties (max 25). MC, VI, AE, Dis. Out-of-town checks OK with ID.

Pinewood Supper Club
Supper club
1208 Halfmoon Lake Dr., Mosinee / 715-693-3180
(Follow Main St. through Mosinee to Cty. KK,
then follow the signs to the restaurant.)

The Pinewood is located on the shore of beautiful Halfmoon Lake. The building dates back to the early part of the century, although additions have been made over the years. This is a classic Wisconsin supper club, serving generous portions of seafood, aged steaks, and fresh fish nightly. Attire is casual and atmosphere is relaxed. **Inexpensive to expensive**. Most dinners $5-22. Serving dinner weekdays 5-10, Fri.-Sat. until 10:30, Sun. 4-9. Parking lot. Wheelchair accessible. Smoking & nonsmoking sections. Cocktail lounge. Children's menu. Reservations recommended. Takeouts. Catering service. Private parties (max. 200). MC, VI, AE, Dis. Out-of-town checks OK with ID.

Friar Tuck's Pub & Grille
American
1147 W. Queen's Way, Nekoosa / 715-325-3338
(On Hwy. 13, 10 mi S of Wisconsin Rapids,
1 mi N of Lake Arrowhead Golf Course)

Friar Tuck's offers a full menu, including broasted chicken, barbecued ribs, steaks, many different hamburgers, and a Friday night fish fry, all in a warm, friendly, and casual atmosphere. Next door to the restaurant is Pizza de Action, owned by the same friendly folks.

Inexpensive to moderate. Most dinners $5-13. Serving Sun. noon-10, Mon.-Fri. 4-10 (5-10 in winter), Sat. noon-10. Parking lot. Wheelchair accessible. No policy on smoking. Full bar. Children's menu. Children's birthday parties at Action de Pizza. Reservations not accepted. Takeouts. Catering service. No credit cards. Out-of-town checks OK with ID.

The Cottage
American / Continental
2900 Post Road, Plover / 715-341-1600

Located in a historic 1861 home, the Cottage offers fine cuisine in a cozy and homelike atmosphere. In warm weather, many diners like to eat on the outdoor balcony. Specialties of the house include beef Wellington, walleyed pike in a bag, onion loaf, and mud pie.

Moderate. Most dinners $10-16. Serving weekdays 11-2 & 5-10, Sat.-Sun. dinner only, 5-10. Parking lot. Wheelchair accessible. Smoking & nonsmoking sections. Cocktail lounge. Children's menu. Reservations recommended. Local delivery & takeouts. Catering service. Private parties (max. 45). All major credit cards.

Bernard's
French / German
701 Second St. N., Stevens Point / 715-344-3365

Bernard's has been serving discriminating diners in Stevens Point for more than two decades. Chef Bernard Kurzawa is best known for his fresh Wisconsin veal dishes, prepared in the Continental manner. Bison is also a staple of the menu, and the Continental pastries are highly recommended. Bernard also does chef's demonstrations for groups, with advance notice.

Moderate to expensive. Most dinners $12-18. Serving dinner weekdays 5-10, Fri. 4:30-10:30, Sat. 5-11, Sun. 4-9 (Easter & Mother's Day from 11:30). Parking lot. Dining area wheelchair accessible (rest rooms soon to be accessible; call). Smoking & nonsmoking sections. Cocktail lounge. Reservations recommended. Live music & dancing Fri. nights. Private parties (max. 400). MC, VI, Dis, DC, CB. No checks.

The Restaurant
Sentry Insurance Headquarters
Italian / American
1800 N. Point Dr., Stevens Point / 715-346-6010
(On the G-2 level of the Sentry Insurance Headquarters Building)

The Restaurant offers an elegant dining experience in the Stevens Point area. The dining room overlooks two meadows with deer feeders that are lit up at night. The view is beautiful, night or day, and the food is excellent and very affordable. There are nine pasta dishes, including shrimp fettucine Alfredo, linguine with baby clams, meat or seafood lasagna, and spaghetti al Caruso (with pan-fried chicken livers and crumbled bacon). The menu also lists three veal dishes, three chicken dishes, and six steaks. Desserts include zabaglione, an Italian custard served over fresh fruit and topped with chocolate. (The Restaurant serves dinner only, but lunch is available at the adjacent Pagliacci Taverna, which also has an Italian menu.)

Inexpensive to moderate. Most dinners $5-15. Serving Mon.-Thurs. 5-10 pm, Fri. & Sat. 5-10. Parking lot. Wheelchair accessible. Smoking & nonsmoking sections. Cocktail lounge/bar. Children's portions. Reservations recommended. Takeouts. Catering service. Private parties (max. 80). MC, VI, AE. No checks.

Silver Coach
American
38 Park Ridge Dr., Stevens Point / 715-341-6588
(From Hwy. 10/51, 3/4 mi W on Hwy. 10)

The Silver Coach, founded in 1945, is a landmark restaurant in Stevens Point, serving fresh, creative, American dishes. The bar is made from a 1905 Smith Barney railroad car. Another feature of the restaurant is a private coach dining room for two to four people. The restaurant is also decorated with artwork from prominent Wisconsin artists. The Silver Coach menu features Cajun specialties, ribs, and desserts made from scratch, all served in a casual and friendly atmosphere.

Moderate: Most dinners $11-16. Serving Mon.-Sat. 5 to closing. (Bar open at 4.) Not wheelchair accessible. Smoking and nonsmoking sections. Cocktail lounge/bar. Children's menu. Reservations recommended. Takeouts. Catering service. Private parties (max. 25). MC, VI. Out-of-town checks OK with ID.

Helen's Kitchen
American
1116 W. Main St., Waupun / 414-324-3441
(From Waupun, W on Hwy. 49. Located in the Park View Plaza.)

Helen's Kitchen was founded in 1976, and ever since has been serving fresh, wholesome foods at modest prices to local folks and tourists alike. People rave about Helen's homemade pies and broasted chicken. There is also a popular Friday night fish fry. This is also a popular place to grab an early morning breakfast, on the way to work, the fishing hole, or the duck blind.

Inexpensive. Most dinners $4-7. Serving Mon.-Fri. 5 am-10:30 pm, Sat. 5 am-9:30 pm. Closed Sun. Parking lot. Wheelchair accessible. Smoking & nonsmoking sections. No alcohol. Children's menu. Seniors discount (age 55+). Reservations recommended for large groups. Takeouts. Private parties (max.70). No credit cards. Out-of-town checks OK with ID.

Mead Inn
Yorkshire Room and Pub
American / International
451 E. Grand Ave., Wisconsin Rapids / 715-423-1500
(On the E side of the Wisconsin River on downtown Hwy. 13/73)

The Mead Inn, owned by Consolidated Papers, Inc., is a good place to eat in Wisconsin Rapids, popular with business people, local residents, and travelers alike. The menu is broad and varied, featuring steaks, seafood, pasta dishes, veal scallopini, prime rib, Gulf shrimp, and daily specials. There are home-style baked goods and desserts, and a Sunday brunch.

Moderate. Most dinners $10-15. Serving Sun. 6:30 am-9:45 pm (brunch 11:30-2), Mon.-Sat. 6:30 am-10:30 pm. Parking lot. Wheelchair accessible. Smoking & nonsmoking sections. Cocktail lounge/bar. Children's menu. Reservations recommended. Live piano, organ, vocals Tues.-Sat. eves. Private parties (max. 375). All major credit cards. Out-of-town checks OK with ID.

The Vintage
Restaurant
3110 Eighth St. S., Wisconsin Rapids / 715-421-4900

The Vintage, building customer loyalty since 1978, is known for its fresh seafood and homemade baked goods. It offers relaxed and casual dining, yet is also popular as a business meeting place.

Moderate to expensive. Most dinners $13-23. Serving Sun. 4:30-9, Mon.-Thurs. lunch 11-2, Fri. 4:30-10, Sat. 5-10. Parking lot. Wheelchair accessible. Smoking & nonsmoking sections. Cocktail lounge. Children's menu. Reservations recommended. Takeouts. Private parties (max. 75). MC, VI, AE. Out-of-town checks OK with ID.

NORTH WOODS
Including Antigo, Boulder Junction, Eagle River, Fifield, Hayward, Hazelhurst, Manitowish Waters, Minocqua/Woodruff, Presque Isle, Rhinelander, Rice Lake, St. Germain, Star Lake, Suring, and Wausau

Leffel's
Supper club
1315 Forest Ave., Antigo / 715-627-7027
(From Hwy. 45, go W on Forest Ave.)

Leffel's is a sterling example of the old-time Wisconsin supper club, featuring a menu stacked with deep-fried seafood, steaks, prime rib, pork chops, and barbequed ribs—the kind of hearty food that both tourists and locals cherish. Leffel's has nightly specials, including Kansas City strip steak on Monday and Tuesday, prime rib on Wednesday, Saturday, and Sunday, and roast Long Island duck on Sunday. Thursday night is German night, featuring wiener schnitzel, sauerbraten, and ribs with sauerkraut, and Friday, of course, offers the famous fish fry—perch or haddock.

Moderate. Most dinners $10-15. Serving Sunday brunch 11-2, weekdays 11-2 & 4:30-10, Fri. 11-2 & 4:30-10, Sat. 4:30-10. Nearby public parking lot. Wheelchair accessible. No policy on smoking. Cocktail lounge/bar. Children encouraged. Children's menu and parties. Reservations recommended. Takeouts and local deliveries. Live entertainment Saturday nights. Private parties (max. 100). MC. Out-of-town checks OK with ID.

The Guide's Inn
Supper club
Hwy. M, Boulder Junction / 715-385-2233

Boulder Junction, once a rich logging center, is now in the heart of one of Wisconsin's most popular tourist areas. The Guide's Inn, serving both local people and tourists since 1936, is noted for its fine cuisine and relaxed north woods atmosphere. Pan-fried walleye, beef Wellington, shrimp St. James, roast duck, several veal dishes, blackened steaks, seafood, and pasta enliven the menu. All foods are prepared under the direction of owner-chef "Jimmy Dean" Van Rossum, a member of the American Culinary Federation. Everything is homemade, here, including the breads, spreads, soups, and desserts.

Moderate. Most dinners $11-16. Serving dinner daily 5-10. Parking lot. Wheel chair accessible. Smoking & nonsmoking sections. Cocktail lounge. Children's portions. Reservations recommended for parties of 6 or more. MC, VI. Out-of-town checks OK with ID.

The Chanticleer Inn
Supper club
1458 E. Dollar Lake Rd., Eagle River / 715-479-4486

This little resort complex, three miles east of Eagle River off Hwy. 70, includes a motel, suites, cottages, villas, and condominiums, as well as one of the best restaurants in the area. Located in Vilas County lake country, the restaurant offers great views of the water. It's also on a snowmobile trail. The inn has been going since 1951, and under its present ownership since 1972. Chicken kiev, served daily, is a specialty of the house, along with prime rib, which is served Wednesdays and Saturdays.

Moderate to expensive. Most dinners $8-18. Serving dinner *mid-June to Labor Day* 5:30-9:30 daily. *Labor day to mid-June*, dinner Mon., Wed., Thurs. 5:30-8:30, Fri.-Sat. until 9:30. Closed Tues. Parking lot. Wheelchair accessible. No policy on smoking. Cocktail lounge. Children's menu. Takeouts. Private parties (max. 100). MC, VI, AE, Dis, DC. Out-of-town checks OK with ID.

The Copper Kettle
Family restaurant / Supper club
207 E. Wall St., Eagle River / 715-479-4049
(In downtown Eagle River)

This is Eagle River's premier family restaurant, with a twelve-page menu offering something for absolutely everyone. For heavy eaters, there is the $3.95 all-you-can-eat pancake special—and if you do well, you can enter the "Pancake Hall of Fame" and have your name printed in the next menu. Champion Jeff Prostek ate 30 pancakes. Can you? For light eaters, including both junior and senior citizens, there is a special low-price menu. For everyone, there are hearty breakfasts, including twelve omelets, potato pancakes, huevos a la Mexicana, waffles, shrimp 'n eggs, corn fritters, and eggs Benedict. Lunchtime brings homemade soups and chili, sandwiches, and burgers. Dinner, which is served from 11 am, includes such staples as deep-fried shrimp, steaks, walleye filets, liver and onions, and pork chops. Stars of the dessert tray include peanut butter pie, and hot caramel apple pie. The cooking isn't fancy at the Copper Kettle, but the food is good, there's lots of it, and the prices are reasonable. A great place to take the kids.

Inexpensive to moderate. Most dinners $6-12. Serving daily 6 am-9 pm. Nearby parking. Wheelchair accessible. Smoking & nonsmoking sections. Cocktail lounge/bar. Children's menu. Reservations not needed. MC, VI. Out-of-town checks OK with ID.

The Pasta Cottage
Italian
1265 Catfish Lake Rd., Eagle River / 715-479-2388
(Just off Hwy. 70, about 2 mi from Eagle River)

For great pizza, folks in this north woods area head for the Pasta Cottage. This is homemade pan-style pizza, made to order. It takes some time to make, so be sure to call ahead if you're in a hurry, or you want it to carry back to the cabin. But you might want to stay and enjoy the other Italian specialties—veal parmesan, tortellini, spaghetti with meatballs, homemade ravioli, stuffed jumbo shells, or linguine with white clam sauce. There are also antipasto salads, Italian sandwiches, and specials for lighter appetites. All this is served in a casual, north woods atmosphere with a great view. Kids love it.

Inexpensive. Most dinners $7-10. Serving Sun. 4-9, other days 4-10. (Closed Tues.) Parking lot. Wheelchair accessible. No policy on smoking. Cocktail lounge/bar. Children's portions. Reservations recommended. Takeouts. (No delivery.) Catering service. Private parties (max. 60). MC, VI. Out-of-town checks OK with ID.

Hicks' Landing
Supper club
N12888 Hicks Rd., Fifield / 715-762-5008
(From Hwy. 13, E 1-1/2 mi on Hwy. 70, S 3-1/2 mi on Hicks Rd.)

This renowned supper club overlooks the Sailor Creek Flowage in the Chequamegon National Forest. It was founded in 1951 by Francis and Erma Hicks and is still run by Erma. The restaurant is well known for its steaks, lobster, prime rib, barbequed ribs, and scallops, but it is even more famous for its super relish tray. The tray—a two- or three-tier lazy susan—is brought to every table where complete dinners have been ordered. It contains items such as homemade salads, deviled eggs, herring, fresh fruit, home-baked beans—up to 25 items in all! Each table also receives a bowl of greens and homemade dressings. Home-baked breads, garlic toast, soup, home-cut potatoes, and dessert are also included with every complete dinner. And if someone in your party is celebrating a birth-day, just whisper the news to the hostess and a birthday cake with sparklers will appear at dessert time. Hicks' Landing is the very embodiment of north woods hospitality—and a big part of that hospitality is seeing that nobody goes away hungry! You'll be a happy camper at Hicks' Landing.

Inexpensive to expensive. Most dinners $8-19. Seniors & children's dinners under $5. Serving Sun. noon-9, Tues.-Sat. 5-10. Closed Mon. except holidays (noon-9). Parking lot. Wheelchair accessible. Smoking & nonsmoking sections. Cocktail lounge/bar. Children's menu. Reservations not accepted. Occasional live entertainment. MC, VI. Out-of-town checks OK with ID.

Tony's Fireside
Supper club / Steakhouse
Rt. 2, Box 2128, Hayward / 715-634-2710
(From Hwy. 27, go 5 minutes E on Cty. Hwy. K)

The Fireside has been entertaining north woods visitors since 1932, and has been under the ownership of Tony Volpendesto since 1969. The building, located on the Lac Court Oreilles Reservation, dates back to 1884. Tony's menu is loaded with steaks, chops, fish and seafood, pork, and chicken dishes. Some of the house specialties are roast duck, shrimp on a skewer, walleye filet, pork tenderloin, Oriental chicken, shrimp de jonghe, and torsk, which is cod poached and served with drawn butter, Norwegian-style. Dinners, in north woods fashion, include your choice of pasta, wild rice blend or potato; soup, juice or salad; and relish tray. You won't come away hungry after a trip to Tony's Fireside.

Moderate. Most dinners $9-15. Serving Sun. 4:30-9, other days 4:30-10. Closed Mon. Parking lot. Wheelchair accessible. Smoking & nonsmoking sections. Cock-tail lounge/bar. Menu items for light appetites. Reservations recommended. Pri-vate parties (max. 70). MC, VI. Out-of-town checks OK with ID.

★ ★ ★
Jacobi's of Hazelhurst
American & Continental gourmet
9820 Cedar Falls Rd., Hazelhurst / 715-356-5591
(From Hwy. 51, turn W at the Amoco station in Hazelhurst
and go 1/4 mi to restaurant)

Here, in the heart of the north woods, is one of the finest gourmet restaurants in Wisconsin. Allen and Pam Jacobi took an ordinary Wisconsin supper club, in 1972, and gradually turned it into a truly fine dining establishment. The inn was built in 1938, although the back bar dates to 1904. It was here, in a more gracious era, that visitors waited for the "Hiawatha Special" train that brought tourists north to pine forests and fresh air. Appetizers on the Jacobi menu include fiery coconut shrimp, and cream cheese-filled jalapeno peppers. Cashew chicken and Szechwan shrimp are among the entrees, but the specialties of the house include pork Normandy, medallions of veal with sun-dried tomatoes, sweet bourbon ribs, and pasta a la mer (salmon and clams in a thick vegetable stock served over angel hair pasta). But first-time visitors to Jacobi's should certainly try the garlic-stuffed tenderloin (pan-broiled in olive oil and dressed with a Dijon mustard-and-cognac sauce) or the steak au poivre, which is a beef tenderloin encrusted in cracked peppercorns and dressed with a contrasting brandy-cream sauce. Both dishes are truly exciting. The mere memory of them will make you long for Jacobi's, long after your vacation has ended. For more traditional diners, there is also a variety of chicken, steak, and seafood dishes, all done to perfection at this exceptional restaurant.

Moderate to expensive. Most dinners $11-17. *Summer hours:* 4:30-10 daily. *Winter hours:* Sun. 4:30-9, Wed.-Thurs. 4:30-9, Fri.-Sat. 4:30-10. Closed Mon.-Tues. in winter. Off-road parking. Not wheelchair accessible. Totally nonsmoking. Cocktail lounge/bar. Small children not encouraged. Reservations essential in summer and on weekends. MC, VI. Out-of-town checks OK with ID.

Blue Bayou Inn
Creole-Cajun-Louisianan
Hwy. 51, Manitowish Waters
715-543-2537 or 1-800-533-9671
(20 mi N of Minocqua/Woodruff, at Spider Lake Bridge)

Here's a little bit of the Deep South, transported all the way to the north woods. Chef Walter Mazur spent eight years in New Orleans, where he fell in love with the local cuisine. Now, the talented former Chicagoan calls Manitowish Waters home, fortunately for all his loyal north woods clientele. The romantic restaurant, paneled in knotty pine, offers spectacular views of the pine-lined waters of Lake

Manitowish. In summer, cocktails are served on a terrace overlooking the lake. And, if you make arrangements ahead of time, you can have a cocktail cruise aboard the Bayou Queen, Mazur's pontoon boat. The menu offers Louisiana heaven—blackened catfish, Bayou seafood gumbo, crawfish etoufee, Cajun creole, jambalaya, roast duck Cajun style, and, occasionally, alligator bits. There are also a few non-Louisiana dishes, including lobster tail, chicken, and steak. You can even bring in your own fresh fish catch of the day and have Walter prepare it for you, just the way you like it. Or, for that very special occasion, you can arrange to dine with Walter himself. (Allow three and one-half hours for the eight-to-ten-course meal, and wear loose-fitting clothes and an expandable belt.) The Blue Bayou is certainly a unique restaurant in Wisconsin's north woods, well worth a visit.

Expensive. Most dinners $14-25. Serving lunch in Jun., Jul., & Aug. noon-2, Tues.-Sat. Serving dinner from late Apr. thru Oct. 5-10:30, Mon.-Sat. Closed Sun. except holiday weekends. Closed in winter. Parking lot. Wheelchair accessible. Smoking & nonsmoking sections. Cocktail lounge/bar. Children's menu. Children's birthday parties. Reservations recommended (essential weekend eves. in summer). Takeouts. Catering service. Live harp music, Fri.-Sat. eves. MC, VI, Dis. Checks OK with backing of credit card.

Swanberg's Bavarian Inn
German
County Trunk W, Manitowish Waters / 715-543-2122
(In downtown Manitowish Waters)

Boaters and anglers on the Manitowish Chain of Lakes often stop by Swanberg's, a Vilas County landmark since 1940. It's accessible by boat in the summer, on snowmobile in winter (on Trail No. 6). There is fine German- style dining here, with a cozy fireplace and lots of wiener schnitzel, beef rouladen, steaks, and seafood. Greg Swanberg also promises plenty of hot homemade soups and tempting desserts.

Inexpensive to Expensive. Most dinners $7-25. Serving Sun.-Thurs. 11:30-9, Fri.-Sat. until 10. Parking lot. Wheelchair accessible. Smoking & nonsmoking sections. Cocktail lounge. Children's menu. Reservations recommended. Takeouts. Private parties (max. 45). MC, VI, Dis. Out-of-town checks OK with ID.

Voss' Birchwood Lodge
American
Hwy. 51, Manitowish Waters / 715-543-8441
(18 mi N of Minocqua, on Spider Lake)

The Voss family has owned and operated the Birchwood Lodge since 1910. Here, you can return to a bygone era of slow-paced elegance. Combining a rustic atmosphere with modern conveniences, Voss' offers lakeside cottages, a suite of rooms in the main lodge, water activity (including great musky fishing), colorful woods, and superb dining. Breakfast and evening dinner is served in the main dining room of the lodge. A delightful luncheon is served in the Old Settler's Inn in the Chalet building, which also houses an art gallery, gift shop, and antique gallery. The menu changes nightly and features many roasts, broiled steaks, lamb, turkey, corned beef, sweetbreads, calf's liver, shrimp, scallops, and other seafoods and fresh fish entrees. There is always a choice of two vegetables, two potatoes, two salads, and, of course, tempting desserts.

Moderate to expensive. Most dinners $12-18. Serving dinner daily 5:30-8. Parking lot. Dining area wheelchair accessible (but not rest rooms). Smoking & nonsmoking sections. Full bar. Children's portions. Reservations recommended. Private parties (max. 100). No credit cards. Out-of-town checks OK with ID.

Bosacki's Boat House
American
Hwy. 51, Minocqua / 715-356-5292
(In downtown Minocqua)

If there was ever a north woods landmark, Bosacki's is it. Few people have driven through Minocqua more than a couple of times without at least stopping for a Bosacki's ice cream cone. The restaurant has been in the family since 1917, and aims to provide complete service for visitors and local folks alike. There is a tackle shop filling all fishing needs. There are boat rentals, boat docking and fueling, a candy shop-ice cream parlor-arcade room. In winter, Bosacki's serves the snowmobiling crowd. The food here ranges from hamburgers, Reuben sandwiches to prime rib, all-you-can-eat fish fries (Wednesday and Friday nights), and tempting homemade desserts, including hot fudge sundaes and fresh fruit cocktails served at Bosacki's 1903 Brunswick bar. There is always a lively crowd at Bosacki's, and during summer the crowd can be large, so be sure to call ahead (except on Friday, when reservations are not accepted).

Inexpensive to moderate. Most dinners $8-15. Serving daily 11 am-midnight. Sun. brunch 9-1, Oct-May. Parking lot. Not wheelchair accessible. Smoking & nonsmoking sections. Cocktail lounge/bar. Children's portions. Children's birthday parties. Reservations recommended (ex. Fri.). Takeouts. Private parties (max. 40). MC, VI, AE, DC, CB. No checks.

Ma Bailey's
Supper club
8591 Woodruff Rd., Woodruff / 715-356-6133
(From Hwy. 51, E 2 mi on Cty. Rd. J, S 1 mi on Woodruff Rd.)

The history is shady, the Lake Minocqua setting is spectacular, the dinner music is sentimental, and the food is sumptuous—just another evening at Ma Bailey's! When John and Judy Allen bought the "old Ma Bailey place" in 1989, they didn't know exactly what kind of business Ma was running back in the 1920s. But the local folks soon filled them in, and that's why the daily fish special is now known as "The Happy Hooker." The decor recalls the roaring twenties and fabulous thirties, when Chicago gangsters were known to frequent the place. Today, diners come for specialties such as Dolly's Delectable Duck, Boom-Boom's Barbecued Ribs, Katie's Catfish, and Lulu's Lasagne. There are also great steaks, pork chops, shrimp, fresh fish, and chicken dishes. There is a "Light Fantastic" portion of the menu, and wonderful desserts, including the infamous "Bailey Brownie." John plays the piano nightly, Judy can occasionally be coaxed into singing, and in general everyone has a wonderful time. Come by car, boat, or snowmobile.

Inexpensive to moderate. Most dinners $6-15. Serving daily in summer from 5 pm (ex. closed Wed.). Serving in winter Thurs.-Sun. from 5 pm (closed Mon.-Wed.). Parking lot. Wheelchair accessible. Smoking & nonsmoking sections. Cocktail lounge/bar. Children's portions. Children's birthday parties. Reservations recommended. Private parties (max. 90). MC, VI. Out-of-town checks OK with ID.

Carlin Club Lodge
Supper club / German
HC1, Box 385, Presque Isle
715-686-2255 or 1-800-562-5900

In this northern fisherman's paradise, close to the Michigan border, you'll find the Carlin Club. This German restaurant is so far north, in fact, they have Oktoberfest in August! The lodge and rathskeller restaurant, orginally built in the 1940s as a private club, is perched on Carlin Lake. It features north woods lodge decor and a full menu that will take you right back to the Black Forest—pork shank, wiener schnitzel, rahm schnitzel, sauerbraten, knackwurst, bratwurst, sauerkraut, dumplings, and noodles galore. Of course, there are some light entrees, too, including Canadian walleyed pike, roast duckling, porterhouse steak, and sauteed scallops—just in case you're on a diet. Things really begin to swing during Oktoberfest, when Johnny Wagner and his Bavarian Show Band strike up, usually starting the second week in August. Directions? From Hwy. 51, take County Hwy. W east for 12 miles, then south on County Hwy. P for 3 miles, and there you are. Willkommen!

Moderate. Most dinners $10-13. Serving dinner Sun. & weekdays 5-9, Fri.-Sat. 5-10. Parking lot. Wheelchair accessible. Smoking & nonsmoking sections. Cocktail lounge. Children's menu. Reservations recommended. Takeouts. Private parties (max. 40). MC, VI, AE, Dis. Out-of-town checks OK with ID.

Al-Gen Dinner Club
Supper club
3428 Faust Lake Rd., Rhinelander / 715-362-2230
(Just off Business Hwy. 8 East)

The Al-Gen, founded in 1928 and under its new ownership since June, 1993, is housed in a rustic old log cabin, providing a great north woods atmosphere. There is a traditional supper club menu, including excellent barbecued ribs and steaks. There is also a popular fish fry on Friday nights.

Inexpensive to moderate. Most dinners $6-14. Serving Sun. 5-9 pm, Tues.-Sat. 5-10. Closed Mon. Parking lot. Wheelchair accessible. Smoking & nonsmoking sections. Cocktail lounge/bar. Children's menu. Reservations recommended. Takeouts. MC, VI, Dis. Out-of-town checks OK with ID.

Rhinelander Cafe & Pub
Supper club
33 N. Brown St., Rhinelander / 715-362-2918
(In downtown Rhinelander)

Rhinelander's oldest supper club, founded in 1911, is still being run by the same family. Pete Vlahakis and his son Mike are now at the helm, still serving wonderful supper club food. Prime rib, roast duck, and roast lamb are the specialties of the house.

Inexpensive to moderate. Most dinners $8-12. Serving Sun. 7 am-10:30 pm, Mon.-Sat. 7 am-11 pm. Nearby public parking lot. Wheelchair accessible. Smoking & nonsmoking sections. Cocktail lounge/bar. Children's & seniors' portions. Takeouts. MC, VI, Dis. Wisconsin checks OK with ID.

Three Coins Restaurant
at Holiday Acres
American
On Lake Thompson, Rhinelander / 715-369-1500
(From Rhinelander, E 4 mi on Business Hwy. 8)

The Three Coins Restaurant is part of a popular resort and conference center, run by the Blaesing-Zambon family for more than sixty years. From a beginning of a few cottages, the complex has grown over the years to include 28 deluxe cottages, 28 lodge rooms, a coffee shop, a banquet and meeting room, recreational facilities, and, of course, the well-known restaurant, which was begun in 1949. The dining room has a distinct north woods flavor, with plenty of pine, cedar, and stonework (including indoor waterfalls and a fireplace) and also plenty of elegance, with crisp table linen. Diners are afforded beautiful views of the surrounding countryside and of Lake Thompson. The menu is broad, offering a variety of steaks, seafood, and fresh fish specials. There is a Friday Holiday Buffet and a Sunday-in-the-Country breakfast.

Moderate. Most dinners $8-17. Serving Sun. 9-1:30 (brunch) & 5-10, Mon.-Sat. 5-10. Parking lot. Wheelchair accessible. Smoking & nonsmoking sections. Cocktail lounge/bar. Children's menu. Children's birthday parties. Reservations recommended. Live music & dancing Fri. & Sat. eves. (more often in summer). Private parties (max. 200). MC, VI, DC, CB. Out-of-town checks OK with ID.

Lehman's
Supper club
2911 S. Main St., Rice Lake / 715-234-2428
(From Hwy. 53, Exit #140, E on Cty. Rd. O, then S 1 blk on Cty. Rd. SS)

This well-known supper club, founded in 1934, is now run by the third generation of the Lehman family. The menu lists a full selection of traditional entrees, with an emphasis on steaks (hand-cut in the kitchen) and homemade soups. Family-style dinners are served on Sundays, and on Thursday, Saturday, and Sunday evenings, the Lehmans serve complimentary popovers to their guests.

Moderate to expensive. Most dinners $10-18. Serving Sun. 11-9:30, Mon.-Thurs. 11-10, Fri.-Sat. 11-10:30. Parking lot. Wheelchair accessible. Smoking & nonsmoking sections. Cocktail lounge/bar. Children's portions. Reservations recommended. Takeouts. Catering service. Occasional live music. Private parties (max. 200). MC, VI, AE, DC. Out-of-town checks OK with ID.

Clear View Supper Club
Supper club
8599 N. Big St. Germain Dr., St. Germain / 715-542-3474
(On Big St. Germain Lake, between Hwy. 155 & Cty. Rd. C)

This family operated supper club has been serving hungry north woods visitors since 1920. It is an authentic log lodge, with a cozy fireplace and a wonderful view of Big St. Germain Lake. There is a full supper club menu, with barbecued ribs, roast duck, prime rib, steaks, lobster, and much more. As in most other restaurants in pine country, the atmosphere is decidedly casual and relaxed, the service friendly. It's a good place to bring the kids.

Moderate. Most dinners $9-14. Serving Wed.-Mon. 4:30 to close. Closed Tues. Parking lot. Wheelchair accessible. No policy on smoking. Cocktail lounge/bar. Children's menu. MC, VI. Out-of-town checks OK with ID.

Hintz's North Star Lodge
Supper club
Cty. Rd. K, Star Lake / 715-542-3600

This casual restaurant, which dates to 1894, has been under its present ownership since 1980. It is a National Registry building, restored to its original rustic appearance. The dining room offers nice views of Star Lake, and is positioned for great sunsets. The North Star Lodge has a good and imaginative salad bar, a great selection of homemade pies, and a full supper club menu, including some outstanding fresh fish and seafood entrees. Specialties include broiled walleye, steamed shrimp, walleye stuffed with cream cheese, marinated steak, fried chicken, and Lumber Camp Liver. There are also daily specials, including pot roast with carrots, potatoes, cabbage, and lots of dark brown gravy on Tuesday nights. But don't forget to save room for pie! This has long been a favorite place for visitors and local folks alike—a casual and friendly place that offers good food and solid value. You'll like it

Inexpensive to moderate. Most dinners $9-15. Serving dinner daily 5-9 in season. Weekends only, out of season. Parking lot. Wheelchair accessible. Totally nonsmoking. Cocktail lounge/bar. Children's menu. Reservations recommended. No credit cards. Out-of-town checks OK.

Boarding House
Supper club
632 Main St., Suring / 414-842-2884
(On Hwy. 32, in Suring)

You can miss the Boarding House if you drive through town too fast, so look for a brown Victorian building with rose and pink trim. The building dates to 1896, and was indeed once a boarding house (also a hotel and a tavern). It has been renovated and furnished with period antiques. Once inside, you won't need the legendary "boarding house reach," because the friendly staff will serve your very own fine meal—your choice of some of the best prime rib, steaks, and seafood in the region. The Boarding House also features homemade soups, salad dressings, and desserts. There is an extensive salad bar.

Inexpensive to moderate. Most dinners $8-12. Serving Sun. 4-9, Fri. 5-10, Sat. 4-10. (Weekday serving hours vary with the season.) Nearby public parking lot. Wheelchair accessible. Smoking & nonsmoking sections. Cocktail lounge/bar. Children's portions. Reservations not accepted. MC, VI. Out-of-town checks OK with ID.

Michael's Supper Club
Continental / American
2901 Rib Mountain Dr., Wausau / 715-842-9856
(From Hwy. 51, Exit Cty. Rd. N, N 1-1/2 mi)

This fine supper club, founded in 1978, is a favorite with both local residents and visitors to the nearby Rib Mountain ski area and state park. The menu features fresh fish and seafood, veal dishes, pasta specialties, prime rib, and great steaks.

Moderate. Most dinners $12-16. Serving Mon.-Sat. 5-10. Closed Sun. Parking lot. Dining area wheelchair accessible (but not rest rooms). Smoking & nonsmoking sections. Cocktail lounge/bar. Children's menu. Reservations recommended. Private parties (max. 80). All major credit cards. Out-of-town checks OK with ID.

LAKE SUPERIOR SHORE
Including Bayfield, Madeline Island, Superior, and Washburn

Greunke's
American / Cafe
17 Rittenhouse Ave., Bayfield / 1-800-245-3072

Greunke's is one of the cherished institutions of the North Country, located in a historic 1863 building that long served as a country inn, and has now served as a restaurant since 1941. The menu spans the full range of American foods, but Greunke's is especially proud of its Trout Hemingway—sesame seed breaded lake trout in a lemon-lime butter sauce—which was featured in a 1984 issue of *Bon Appetit* magazine. The homemade soups and fruit pies are also very popular with customers—especially the fresh raspberry pie. There is a nightly fish boil in summer, including whitefish, red potatoes, coleslaw, and rye bread. In this little Lake Superior fishing village, Greunke's is quite a catch.

Inexpensive to moderate. Most dinners $8-15. *Serving April through October only.* Sun.-Thurs. 7 am-9 pm, Fri.-Sat. until 10. Summer fish boils 6-7 pm. Parking lot. Dining room wheelchair accessible (but not rest rooms). Smoking & nonsmoking sections. Beer & wine. Children's menu. Children's birthday parties. Private parties (max. 35). MC, VI, Dis, DC, CB. Out-of-town checks OK with ID.

Maggie's Restaurant
Cafe
257 Manypenny, Bayfield / 715-779-5641

When it comes to fun restaurants, Maggie's takes a back seat to nobody. This is a small, unpretentious cafe with a lighthearted atmosphere and a wry sense of humor about itself. At last count, for example, there were 268 flamingos adorning the walls and ceiling, says manager Janel Ryan. A model train circles the dining area to amuse diners. And all this is not to take your mind off the food, because it is really good. The specialty burgers, black beans and rice, fajitas, ethnic dinners, and specials are all made from scratch, in house. A specialty not to be missed are the whitefish livers. In the summer (granted, a brief window in Bayfield) Maggie's has a canvas-covered outdoor deck for cocktails and hors d'oeuvres.

Inexpensive to moderate. Most dinners $7-14. *Summer hours:* Sun.-Thurs. 6 am-11 pm, Fri.-Sat. 6 am-midnight. *Winter hours:* Sun.-Thurs. 6 am-9 pm, Fri.-Sat. 6 am-10 pm. Parking lot. Dining area is wheelchair accessible (but not rest rooms). No policy on smoking. Full bar. Children's menu. Seniors discount (age 65+). Reservations not accepted. Takeouts. MC, VI. Out-of-town checks OK with ID.

★ ★ ★

The Old Rittenhouse Inn
Gourmet regional cuisine
301 Rittenhouse Ave., Bayfield / 715-779-5111

The Rittenhouse is one of the most beautiful, best known, and most photographed inns in the Great Lakes region. It also prides itself on the most imaginative and well-prepared regional cuisine in the Upper Midwest. It is housed in a Victorian mansion, studded with antiques, wood-burning fireplaces, and splendid views of Lake Superior. Dinners, all served at a fixed price, include six courses, which are announced and explained by the server. There is no printed menu. Included is a choice of soup, salad, and entree, with side dishes of vegetables and relishes, and dessert. Dinner is served leisurely, over a two to two and one-half hour period. Fresh, regional foods of the season are emphasized—wild blueberry marmalade, apple-glazed pork chops, fresh Lake Superior whitefish, and lake trout fillets prepared in a number of ways. Wild leeks, morel mushrooms, fiddlehead ferns, and other local plants, both wild and domestic, often find their way into the creative Rittenhouse recipes. A typical dinner might include a French fruit soup featuring fresh Bayfield raspberries and Gewurztraminer wine, and smoked trout salad with wild rice, cheddar cheese, chives, and dill, served with a horseradish and lemon sauce. The entree might be veal paprikash, brandied chicken breasts, or grilled whitefish with red pepper butter. And for dessert? How about pumpkin-walnut pie, Wisconsin cheese pie, Bayfield strawberry mousse, or red raspberry truffles? The menu changes constantly, depending on the fresh foods available at the time and the inspiration of the chef. Whatever the particular night's offerings, you may be sure that your dining experience will be a memorable one at the Old Rittenhouse Inn. You might even want to buy a copy of the Rittenhouse cookbook.

Expensive: Fixed price, $37.50 per person, plus tax and gratuity. Fixed price, lunch, $13.50 plus tax and gratuity. Serving Sunday brunch Memorial Day to October, 11-1:30. Weekday dinner Memorial Day to October. Saturday and Sunday dinner served year 'round. Call for hours and reservations, which are essential. Parking lot. Wheelchair accessible. Totally nonsmoking. Beer & wine served. Children's portions at half-price. Private parties (max. 48). MC, VI. Out-of-town checks OK with ID.

The Pier Plaza
Cafe
City Dock on the Waterfront, Bayfield / 715-779-3330

The Johnson family has owned and run the Pier Plaza since 1954, and John and Sharon Johnson can still promise the best view of Lake Superior of any restaurant around. The home cooking is good, too, featuring some mighty fine soups, chili, fresh fish, delicious desserts, and baked goods warm from the oven.

Inexpensive to moderate. Most dinners $7-11. Serving daily. Parking lot. Wheelchair accessible. Smoking & nonsmoking sections. Beer & wine served. Children's menu. Children's birthday parties arranged. Special "early bird" prices. Takeouts. MC, VI. Out-of-town checks OK with ID.

★ ★ ★

The Clubhouse on Madeline Island
American / Regional
La Pointe, Madeline Island / 715-747-2612
(Take the ferry from Bayfield; complimentary Clubhouse shuttle from ferry dock to restaurant)

Some of Wisconsin's very best restaurants are in out-of-the-way places, and here is a prime example. Owner Mary Rice set out in 1983 to create something beyond the ordinary on this northernmost Wisconsin outpost. "I wanted to combine distinct northern Wisconsin food with high-class French in a special setting that wasn't stuffy," she once told *Midwest Living* magazine. The result of her efforts is sure to please. The menu, supervised by executive chef Jim Webster, changes every two or three weeks, but typical appetizers might include grilled shrimp with wild rice risotto cake, plum-cranberry chutney, and citrus sauce, or herb-cured Atlantic salmon with basil-scented sweet potato salad, creme fraiche, and focaccia toast. Entrees could include roast lake trout on braised savory cabbage with cucumber-dill salad and mustard sauce, or sauteed walnut-crusted Lake Superior whitefish, or roast boneless lamb loin with grilled Japanese eggplant, oven-dried tomatoes, crispy goat cheese and chive-stuffed potatoes, and minted sherry almond sauce. Desserts include raspberry Napoleon with caramel custard and raspberry sauce, and warm chocolate cake with homemade honeyroasted pecan ice cream. Enough? All this is served amid the spectacular sylvan landscape of Madeline Island and the surrounding waters of Lake Superior. The building itself is a 12-sided, glass-walled affair with a panoramic view of the Robert Trent-Jones golf course and the marina. Many special events are scheduled throughout the season.

Expensive. Most dinners $20-29. Serving 6-10 pm daily, May thru Oct.. Parking lot. Wheelchair accessible. Smoking & nonsmoking sections. Cocktail lounge/bar. Reservations recommended. Catering service. Live music and dancing for special events (call for information). MC, VI. Out-of-town checks OK with ID.

The Pub Restaurant
Continental / Regional
La Pointe, Madeline Island / 715-747-6315
(Upon arrival on island, turn right at post office,
go 1 mi to restaurant, next to marina)

The Pub is part of The Inn Resort, which features lakeside condominiums, woodside cottages, and tennis courts for family vacations and business conferences. It is also a short chip away from the Robert Trent-Jones golf course. The Pub specializes in barbeque, grilled lake trout and whitefish and grilled garlic shrimp, along with other Continental and regional dishes.

Moderate to expensive. Most dinners, $8-19. *Summer hours*: Breakfast daily 7-11, lunch 11-2, dinner 5:30-10. Reduced hours (call) rest of year. Closed Nov. through Mar. Nearby parking lot. Dining area wheelchair accessible (but not rest rooms). Smoking & nonsmoking sections. Bar. Children's menu. (Small children not encouraged at dinner.) Reservations recommended. MC, VI, AE. Out-of-town checks OK with ID.

Town Crier Steak, Cake & Seafood House
Colonial American / Family-style
4927 E. Second St., Superior / 715-398-7521
(On Hwys. 2/53, in Colonial Village, in east Superior)

There's a good chance you'll be greeted at this restaurant by the wonderful aroma of baking muffins, which are the specialty of the house. This is a friendly family restaurant with an Early American atmosphere, run by the O'Brien family since 1978. The menu features meals in a skillet (pork chop, chicken, ground beef, steak, or cod, served with a medley of vegetables), steaks, shrimp, barbecued ribs, chicken, seafood, and fresh-water fish, all at modest prices. There are also fourteen sandwiches, homemade chili and clam chowder, and two special casseroles. Comfort food rules at the Town Crier. It's a great place to take the kids.

Inexpensive. Most dinners $6-8. Serving daily 6 am-11 pm. Parking lot. Wheelchair accessible. Smoking & nonsmoking sections. No alcohol. Children's menu. Children's birthday parties. Seniors discount (age 60+). Reservations recommended for large groups. Takeouts. Private parties (max. 40). MC, VI, AE, Dis, DC. Out-of-town checks OK with ID.

Steak Pit
Supper club / Steakhouse
125 Harbor View Dr., Washburn / 715-373-5492
(On the waterfront, overlooking the marina and Lake Superior)

Steaks are the order of the day at the Steak Pit. And we're talking *serious* steaks, here —pure Angus beef, cut and cooked the way you like. This restaurant has been serving 'em that way for more than twenty years, now. The restaurant is also known for its fresh lake trout, whitefish, and walleye, and for its award-winning onion rings and cheesecake. There are also homemade soups, fresh salads, and lighter fare, including hamburgers.

Moderate to expensive. Most dinners $10-18. Serving Sun. 4 to close, Mon.-Sat. 5 to close (usually 10:30). Bar open daily at 4. Parking lot. Wheelchair accessible. Smoking & nonsmoking sections. Cocktail lounge/bar. Reservations recommended. Takeouts. Private parties (max. 300). MC, VI. Out-of-town checks OK with ID.

SOUTHWEST
Including Dodgeville, Fennimore, Hazel Green, Mineral Point, Platteville, and Spring Green

---

Thym's Supper Club
Supper club / Steakhouse
Hwy 23 North, Dodgeville / 608-935-3344
(1 mi N of Dodgeville, 5 mi S of House on the Rock)

Here is a casual, come-as-you-are supper club that serves big steaks and seems made for relaxing. What else could you ask, after a hard day of business or traveling? The menu has all the usual supper club staples—chicken, pork, seafood, and fish—but Thym's is best known for its great steaks, which are hand-cut right in the kitchen. There are also nightly specials, including prime rib, pasta dishes, and stir-fries. "One thing we strive for is to make everyone feel comfortable, whether the guest is wearing formal wear or casual wear," says co-owner Mitch Thym. An attitude we appreciate.

Inexpensive to moderate. Most dinners $7-16. Serving Sun. 10:30-9, Mon.-Fri. 11-10, Sat. dinner 5-10 pm. Parking lot. Wheelchair accessible. Smoking & non-smoking sections. Cocktail lounge/bar. Children's menu. Reservations recom-mended. Takeouts. Private parties (max. 200). MC, VI, AE, Dis, DC. Out-of-town checks OK with ID.

The Silent Woman
Supper club
1096 Lincoln Ave., Fennimore / 608-822-3782

Many travelers will go out of their way to arrange dinner at the Silent Woman, located right in the heart of downtown Fennimore (pop. 2,212), which is located at the intersection of Hwys. 18 and 61, in southwestern Wisconsin. This popular supper club (there is also a coffee shop) serves strictly American-style food. The Victorian courtyard decor is one of the most spectacular of any Wisconsin restaurant, with balconies, bridges, period street lamps, alleys, and overhangs. It's almost like dining in a little town square of long ago. This might also be the only restaurant in the state with trees and plants growing along a small stream that flows through the main dining room. (And no, customers may not fish in the stream.) Seafood and prime rib (blackened or regular) dominate the menu. Favorites include jambalaya, shrimp Dianne, black Angus beef steaks, and authentic Cajun dishes. The Silent Woman's sweet potato pecan pie is a favorite dessert. For a delightful dining experience, the Silent Woman is hard to beat, any place in Wisconsin.

Inexpensive to moderate. Most dinners $9-16. Serving dinner Wed.-Thurs. 5-9, Fri.-Sat. 5-10. Sun. brunch 10-2 in main dining room. Coffee shop open Wed.-Sat. 7 am-2 pm, Sun. 7-10 am. Everything closed Mon.-Tues. Parking lot. Partially wheelchair accessible (call ahead). No policy on smoking. Cocktail lounge. Reservations recommended. Takeouts. Private parties (max. 200). MC, VI, AE.

Wisconsin House Stage Coach Inn
Continental and American cuisine
2105 E. Main St., Hazel Green / 608-854-2233
(1 block E of Hwys. 11/80 on Cty. W)

The Stage Coach Inn, located in a historic 1846 inn, serves a seven-course dinner on Friday and Saturday nights only. There is a fixed menu and a fixed price, and there is only one seating each evening.

Expensive. Dinners range from $16.95 to $19.95. Dinner is served at 7 pm. Lunches are served Tues.-Fri. 11:30-2. Easy curb parking. Not wheelchair accessible. Call for smoking policy. Cocktail lounge/bar. Small children are not encouraged. Reservations are required. MC, VI. Out-of-town checks OK with ID.

Ovens of Brittany at the Chesterfield Inn
American / Cornish
20 Commerce St., Mineral Point / 608-987-3682

The successful Ovens of Brittany, which operates several restaurants in Madison, has been serving traditional Cornish food from the Chesterfield Inn since 1990. The Chesterfield is a beautiful 1834 stone inn built by the Welsh during Wisconsin's early lead mining era. The small dining room seats 35, lending a sense of intimacy to this charming inn. The menu is similar to those in other Ovens of Brittany restaurants, with chicken pot pie, vegetable stir-fries, fresh fish and seafood dishes, homemade soups, and excellent baked goods. But here at the Chesterfield, traditional Cornish specialties are added, in particular the Cornish pasty (rhymes with nasty—but sure doesn't taste that way), which combines meat, potatoes, and, sometimes, vegetables, all wrapped in dough and baked like a pie. The miners carried these complete lunches into the mines with them, and now you can enjoy one in the comfort of the Chesterfield. In all but the coldest months, you'll find it delightful to sit on the outdoor cobblestone terrace of the inn, nestled against a sandstone wall and surrounded by blooming plants. This is truly one of the most enjoyable dining experiences in all of Wisconsin. Don't miss it, when you find yourself in the Mineral Point area. (And if you fall completely in love with the Chesterfield, you'll be happy that it is also an eight-room bed-and-breakfast.)

Moderate. Most dinners $10-15. Inn and restaurant open May thru Oct. only. Serving Sun., Mon. Wed. & Thurs. 8 am-8 pm, Fri. & Sat. 8 am-9 pm. Restaurant closed Tues. Parking lot. Dining area wheelchair accessible (but not rest rooms). Smoking and nonsmoking sections. Full bar. (Also outdoor bar.) Children's menu. Children's birthday parties. Reservations recommended. Local deliveries. Take-outs. Catering service. Private parties. MC, VI, AE. Out-of-town checks OK with ID.

The Timbers
Supper club
670 Ellen St., Platteville / 608-348-2406
(At intersection of Hwys.151 & 80/81)

The Timbers is one of the most renowned supper clubs in Wisconsin, famous for the impressive Timbers organ, which is the largest theater electronic pipe organ ever built. The redwood, stone, and brick restaurant, designed by John W. Steinmann, shows the unmistakable influence of fellow Wisconsin architect Frank Lloyd Wright, capping the brow of a hill and nestled among large old trees. Diners here will find an extensive menu including more than a hundred entrees—poultry, beef, pasta, veal, pork, and more. As an example, there are 29 fish entrees, including haddock, catfish, sole, salmon, walleyed pike, trout, cod, shrimp, lobster, mussels, swordfish, halibut, and scallops. There is a "lighter fare" section of the menu, and specials on weekend nights. Whatever your preference, you're sure to find it at the Timbers.

Moderate to expensive. Most dinners $10-18. Serving Sun. 10:30-2 (brunch) & 3-9, Mon.-Sat. 11-1:30 & 5-10. Parking lot. Wheelchair accessible. Smoking & nonsmoking sections. Cocktail lounge/bar. Children's menu. Reservations requested. Takeouts. Live piano music Fri. & Sat. Live organ music Mon.-Sun. (Entertainment schedule may vary Jan.-Mar.) Private parties (max 200). MC, VI, AE, Dis, DC.

The Post House
American / Supper club
127 E. Jefferson St., Spring Green / 608-588-2595

The Post House dates back to 1857, and has operated under the present ownership since 1963. The cocktail lounge was designed by William Wesley Peters, a student of Frank Lloyd Wright. There is an outdoor seating area for cocktails and garden lunches during the warmer months. The Post House menu is standard American, including roast duck, baked leg of lamb, beef rib roast, baked chicken, and roast turkey. Everything is well prepared and served in cheerful surroundings.

Inexpensive to moderate. Most dinners $8-14. Serving weekdays 11-2 & 5-9, Fri.-Sat. 11-2 & 5-10, Sun. 11-8 (brunch 8-11, Jun. to Oct). Nearby public parking. Dining room wheelchair accessible (but not rest rooms). Smoking & nonsmoking sections. Cocktail lounge. Children's portions. Reservations recommended. Takeouts. Private parties (max. 48). MC, VI. Out-of-town checks OK with ID.

The Round Barn
American
Hwy. 14, Spring Green / 608-588-2568
(8 mi N of House on the Rock, 3 mi N of Taliesin)

The Round Barn was built in 1914 and was used as a dairy barn until 1949, when it was converted to a truck stop. In 1952 it was made into a full-service restaurant, and later 44 lodging rooms were added to the complex. Through a window that used to be a hay chute, in the ceiling of the bar area, patrons can look up fifty feet and see the original roof rafters. The cupola on the restaurant was once the top of a silo. The dining room today is expansive and comfortable, the service is country-friendly and efficient, and the menu offers specialties such as fried chicken, barbecued pork back ribs, Cornish hen, pork chops, and Round Barn Casserole (ham and chicken simmered in a cheddar cheese sauce, over fresh broccoli on toast points). There are four vegetarian dishes, seven seafood selections, and four steaks. There are weekend specials (including a Friday night seafood buffet) and a "lighter side" menu.

Moderate. Most dinners $9-13. *Summer hours*: Sun. 6:30-3 (brunch 10-3) & 4-9, Mon.-Thurs. 6:30-3 & 5-9, Fri. & Sat. 6:30-3 & 5-10. *Winter hours*: Sun. 7-2 (brunch 10-2) & 4-8, Mon.-Thurs. 11-2 & 5-8, Fri. 11-2 & 5-10, Sat. 7-2 & 5-10. Parking lot. Call for wheelchair accessibility. Smoking & nonsmoking sections. Cocktail lounge/bar. Children's menu. Reservations recommended. Takeouts. Private parties (max. 250). MC, VI, AE, Dis, DC. Out-of-town checks OK with ID.

The Springs Resort Dining Room
The Grill on the Green
American / Regional
5857 Golf Course Rd., Spring Green 608-588-7000
(At Cty. Rd. C, near American Players Theatre)

The Springs Resort, opened in 1993, is a celebration of the verdant, rolling Wisconsin countryside. Here, in Frank Lloyd Wright country, is a hotel, golf course, and beautiful dining room looking out to the wooded bluffs beyond, just a stone's throw from the famous American Players Theatre. The Springs, in fact, is a perfect place for a pre-theatre dinner. Entrees include tea-smoked duck, roasted garlic flan, saffron-grilled shrimp, glorious steaks, and accompaniments such as wild mushroom strudel, steamed red potatoes, wild rice, and other foods of the region. The preparation of each dish is exacting, and the presentation is often a work of Black Angus hamburgers, gourmet pizza, and other light items.

Expensive. Most dinners $15-22. (Grill items $2-7.) Dining room serving dinner Tues.-Sun. 5-9. Closed Mon. Grill serving 9-9 daily. Parking lot. Wheelchair accessible. Dining Room is totally nonsmoking. Smoking is permitted in the Grill. Cocktail lounge/bar. Children's birthday parties in the Grill. Reservations recommended (essential Fri. & Sat.). Takeouts from the Grill. Live piano music Fri. & Sat. Catering service. Private parties (max. 500). MC, VI, Dis. Out-of-town checks OK with ID.

The Boatworks / The Haberdashery
American / Pub
Radisson Hotel, 200 Harborview Plaza, La Crosse / 608-784-6680

The Radisson, on the banks of the mighty Mississippi next to the Civic Center, has two excellent restaurants. The Boatworks is a traditional restaurant serving fresh seafood, unique sautéed entrees, an elegant ambiance, and a splendid view of the river. Service includes a tableside bread cart with a variety of breads and toppings, flaming desserts, and creative entrees. The Haberdashery is a turn-of-the-century styled pub and restaurant with a casual and relaxing atmosphere. It serves sandwiches and salads, a daily luncheon buffet, a Monday night Cajun buffet, Wednesday night Italian buffet, and Friday night fish and chicken buffet. On Thursday nights there is live comedy from Scott Hansen's Comedy Gallery, featuring comedians from all over the U.S.

Boatworks: Moderate to expensive. Most dinner entrees $10-18. Serving Mon.-Sat. 6:30-2 & 5:30-11, Sun. 6:30-11:30, brunch 10-2, dinner 5:30-10. Parking lot. Wheelchair accessible. Smoking & nonsmoking sections. Cocktail lounge. Children's menu. Seniors discount (age 55+). Reservations recommended. Takeouts. Catering service. Piano player weekend nights. Private parties (max. 18). All major credit cards. Checks accepted from hotel guests only.

Haberdashery: Moderate. Most dinners $8-15. Serving Mon.-Sat. 11-11. Sun. brunch 10-2, dinner 2-10. Parking lot. Wheelchair accessible. Smoking & non-smoking sections. Cocktail lounge. Children's menu. Seniors discount (55). Reservations recommended. Takeouts. Dancing with live band playing oldies from the '60s & '70s Tues.-Sat. nights. All major credit cards. Checks accepted from hotel guests only.

The Freighthouse
Steakhouse / Supper club
107 Vine St., La Crosse / 608-784-6211

La Crosse is a haven of fine dining and plain good eating, and this is one of the best in the city. The Freighthouse is one of the famous Wisconsin restaurants on the Mississippi River, serving since 1978 in a building that was, indeed, a freighthouse, and is now on the National Register of Historic Places. The Freighthouse is located next to Riverside Park in downtown La Crosse. It suffered a disastrous fire in 1992, but quickly rebuilt to serve its loyal clientele once again. Freighthouse specialties include prime rib and fresh seafood, including what many believe to be the best Alaskan king crab legs to be found anywhere.

Moderate. Most dinners $11-16. Serving Sun. 5-9:30 pm, Mon.-Sat 5:30-10:30 pm. Parking lot. Wheelchair accessible. Smoking & nonsmoking sections. Cocktail lounge. Children encouraged. Reservations not accepted. Takeouts. Acoustic guitar player Fri.-Sat. Private parties (max. 120). All major credit cards. Checks OK with ID.

Gionelli's
Italian-American
200 Main St., La Crosse / 608-782-2323
(Across from the La Crosse Center in downtown La Crosse)

Gionelli's serves a fine selection of traditional Italian-American dishes in historic Powell Place. The decor incorporates some interesting historic artifacts, creating a relaxed but elegant atmosphere. Singers entertain patrons on Thursday, Friday, and Saturday nights, and at Sunday brunch.

Moderate to expensive. Most dinners $8-22. Serving Sun. 10:30 am-10 pm (brunch 10:30-2), weekdays 11-10, Fri. 11-11, Sat. 11-midnight. Nearby parking lot; easy curb parking. Wheelchair accessible. Smoking & nonsmoking sections. Cocktail lounge/bar. Children's portions (of side orders). Local delivery. Takeouts. Catering service. Private parties (max. 200). MC, VI, AE, Dis, DC. Out-of-town checks OK with ID.

Michael's Restaurant
American / Greek
1815 Ward Ave., La Crosse / 608-788-1900
(From I-90, Exit #53, S on Hwys. 53/35 to southern edge of city. Restaurant is on Hwys. 53/35.)

This restaurant is heir to a fine tradition begun by the patriarch of the family, Michael George Pappas, who arrived from Greece and opened his first restaurant in Northfield, Minnesota, in 1907. For a romantic yet moderately priced dinner, you couldn't do much better than Michael's, especially in their dining room (one of four) called "The Wine Cellar," which has private booths and a cozy fireplace. *Trés romantique!* The specialties here are prime rib, Greek dishe, and sinful desserts, including mocha almond fudge pie. There is also a very nice Sunday champagne brunch. Sample entrees include honey-pecan chicken, shrimp stuffed with crab, and barbequed baby back ribs. For lighter appetites, there are burgers, sandwiches, soups, and salads.

Inexpensive to moderate. Most dinners $7-16. Serving Sun. 10:30-8 (brunch 10:30-2), weekdays 11-2 & 4:30-9:30, Fri. 11-2 & 4:30-10, Sat. 4:30-10. Parking lot. Wheelchair accessible. Smoking & nonsmoking sections. Cocktail lounge/bar. Children's menu. Seniors discount at Sun. brunch (age 50+). Reservations always recommended. Takeouts. Catering service. Occasional live entertainment. Dancing on weekends. Private parties (max. 100). MC, VI, AE, DC, CB. Out-of-town checks OK with ID.

★ ★ ★
Piggy's on Front
American// Barbeque
328 S. Front St., La Crosse / 608-784-4877

Piggy's has been named one of the best restaurants in Wisconsin by several newspapers, from the *Los Angeles Times* to the *Milwaukee Journal,* and we gladly add our name to the list. The National Pork Producers Council named Piggy's the National Restaurant of the Year, for 1990. The meats here are slowly hickory-smoked in Piggy's own kitchen, and the barbeque sauce is incomparable. In addition to the prizewinning barbequed pork chops, pork ribs, and beef ribs, there are beautiful steaks, prime rib (also smoked), seafood, chicken entrees, and luncheon specials. Seafood selections include broiled lobster tail, steamed Alaskan king crab, broiled and barbequed shrimp, and ocean fish specialties. There are even low-calorie selections, which will allow you to order one of Piggy's sinfully delicious desserts, including peanut butter pie and Mississippi mud pie. But if you're a first-time visitor, be sure to order barbequed pork chops or ribs, because you'll know you'll be getting the best in Wisconsin, probably the best in the nation. If you take time to notice the surroundings while you're eating, you'll appreciate the rich wood paneling, stained glass, beautiful antiques, elegant chandeliers, and especially the century-old tiger skin back bar. You might also notice that you are on the banks of the mighty Mississippi, as you see a barge pushing past the rear picture window. Piggy's is a fabulous restaurant, certainly one of our favorites in all Wisconsin.

Moderate to expensive. Most dinners $12-18. Serving Sun. 10-10 (breakfast buffet 11-12), Mon.-Thurs. 11-10, Fri. & Sat. 11-11. Parking lot. Wheelchair accessible. Smoking & nonsmoking sections. Cocktail lounge. Children's menu. Salad bar. "Early bird" prices (25% discount) 4-6 pm. Reservations recommeded. Catering service. All major credit cards. Out-of-town checks OK with ID.

Mill Road Cafe
American
219 E. Mill Rd., Galesville / 608-582-4438
(20 mi N of La Crosse)

The Mill Road Cafe is a cozy and romantic restaurant with great views overlooking Beaver Creek. The owners, who are antique buffs, are proud of their "unbelievable dessert case—all fresh and homemade." The menu here also includes vegetarian entrees. Live music is offered on Friday and Saturday nights—folk, bluegrass, and jazz.

Inexpensive. Most dinners $5-7. Serving Sun. brunch 9-2. Weekdays 9-4. Fri.-Sat. 9-11. Parking lot. Dining room wheelchair accessible (but not rest rooms). Totally nonsmoking. Beer & wine served. Children's menu. Local delivery. Takeouts. Catering service. No credit cards. Out-of-town checks OK with ID.

Burnstad's European Cafe
Continental
Hwy. 12 & 16 East, Tomah / 608-372-3277
(Where I-94 divides from I-90; look for billboard directions)

This restaurant is located in Burnstad's European Village, a specialty mall with the flavor of the old world—brick and cobblestone-like walkways, an Amish shop, clothing stores, a flower shop, and other specialty shops. The Cafe features homemade soups, wonderful salads with homemade dressings, and 35 kinds of desserts. Entrees include strip steak chausseur, tournedos a la champignon, shrimp de jonghe, poulet au framboise, and other Continental selections, including several house specialties with pork loin, scallops, and veal. There is also a menu for lighter appetites.

Moderate. Most dinners $10-15. Serving Sun. 8 am-8 pm, Mon.-Sat. 8-9. Parking lot. Wheelchair accessible. Smoking & nonsmoking sections. Beer & wine served. Children's menu. Reservations recommended. Takeouts. MC, VI, AE, Dis, DC. Out-of-town checks OK with ID.

The Carlton
Supper club
309 Superior Ave., Tomah / 608-372-4136
(Off I-90/94, in downtown Tomah, 1 blk from the railroad depot)

Train buffs will be happy at The Carlton, which has a great collection of railroad memorabilia, including photos of Tomah's interesting railroad history. There are paintings and prints of mighty steam engines of the past, and an oak cabinet containing old conductor and waiter uniforms. Railroad artifacts grace the walls, and—what's that?—a whistle from the kitchen indicates that your dinner may be ready to serve! The Carlton is known for its outstanding prime rib, USDA choice tenderloin and rib eye steaks, shrimp, African lobster tail, lake perch, and steamed and deep-fried seafood. Sandwiches and other light fare are served in the Caboose cocktail lounge, where old fashioneds, made the old-fashioned way, are a specialty. You'll have a lot of fun at The Carlton, a good place to make your whistle-stop in the Tomah area.

Inexpensive to moderate. Most dinners $7-15. Serving Tues.-Thurs. 5-10, Fri. 4:30-10, Sat. 5-10. Closed Sun. & Mon. Parking lot. Dining area wheelchair accessible (but not rest rooms). No policy on smoking. Cocktail lounge/bar. Children's portions. Special "early bird" prices Fri. 4:30-6. Reservations recommended. Takeouts. Catering service. Private parties (max. 125). MC, VI. Out-of-town checks OK with ID.

Trempealeau Hotel and Saloon
American
150 Main St., Trempealeau / 608-534-6898
(From the Great River Road, W at stop sign to Mississippi River)

The Trempealeau Hotel dates to 1871. The dining rooms here offer spectacular views of the Mississippi River and Lock & Dam No. 6, all the better to enjoy the hotel's walnut burger (a vegetarian specialty), homemade soups (veggie clam chowder, minestrone, spicy black bean), and desserts (Swedish apple pie, giant chocolate chip cookies, sour cream poppyseed cake). Throughout the summer, the hotel hosts national acts for their outdoor "Stars Under the Stars" concert series. Each Father's Day weekend, the grounds are transformed into Robin Hood's Forest for a Renaissance festival. Fish boils are available for groups of 25 or more, and also in conjunction with Island Girl Cruises out of La Crosse. The Trempealeau Hotel is a fun place to come, any time of year. Make it a planned stop on your way up the Great River Road.

Inexpensive. Most dinners $7-10. Serving in season Mon.-Fri. 11 am-9 pm, Sat. & Sun. 7 am-9 pm (breakfast until 11:30). Closed Halloween to April Fool's Day. Easy curb parking. Dining area wheelchair accessible (but not rest rooms). Smoking allowed in saloon or outside only. Beer garden. Children's birthday parties. Reservations recommended Sat. eves. Takeouts. Catering service. Live music Sat. eve. (rock, blues, folk, jazz, reggae, country-rock). Dancing anytime. MC, VI. Out-of-town checks OK with ID.

Westby House
American
200 W. State St., Westby / 608-634-4112
(1/2 blk W of Hwys. 14/61/27 in downtown Westby)

The Westby House is an 18-room 1890s Queen Anne home with original stained glass, elegant interior woodwork, period lighting fixtures, and fireplaces. It offers elegant overnight accommodations as well as the restaurant, whose antique-filled dining area occupies three rooms of the main floor. Provincial-style entrees are featured, and—weather permitting—desserts and drinks are served on the veranda. Dinner specialties include sauteed shrimp (sauteed with crab in a garlic-butter sauce), scallops baked in lemon herb butter, Chicken Breast All' Alba (with sauteed mushrooms and mozzarella cheese, served on garlic noodles). There is a tempting lunch menu, too, and wonderful homemade desserts.

Moderate. Most dinners $10-15. Serving weekdays 10-3, Fri. 10-8, Sat. 8 am-9 pm, Sun. 8-3. Parking lot. Wheelchair accessible. Smoking & nonsmoking sections. Full bar. Children's menu. Children's birthday parties. Reservations recommended. Takeouts. Catering service. Private parties (max. 65). MC, VI. Out-of-town checks OK with ID.

Burgundy's / Holiday Inn Gateway
American
1202 W. Clairemont Ave., Eau Claire / 715-834-3181

A favorite place for both business and family travelers in Eau Claire, Burgundy's has been pleasing customers since 1963. Specialties of the house include buffets and great prime rib.

Inexpensive to expensive. Most dinners $8-22. Serving daily 6 am-10 pm. Parking lot. Wheelchair accessible. Smoking & nonsmoking sections. Cocktail lounge. Children's menu. Children's birthday parties. 10% seniors discount. Reservations recommended. Takeouts. Private parties (max. 400). All major credit cards. Checks OK with ID.

★ ★ ★

Fanny Hill Inn & Dinner Theatre
Continental
3919 Crescent Ave., Eau Claire
715-836-8184 or 1-800-292-8026

Fanny Hill is more than a restaurant. It's a weekend! Nestled into a hillside overlooking the Chippewa River Valley, Fanny Hill offers award-winning dining, comedy dinner theatre, and charming bed and breakfast rooms. A beautiful deck and floor-to-ceiling windows in the dining room provide a breathtaking view of the Chippewa River. The decor changes with the seasons, and includes thousands of lights in the elegant Victorian holiday theme, November through January. The menu features a wide variety of cuisine, with flavors and sauces from around the world. And everything is made from scratch. This is truly one of Wisconsin's outstanding restaurants, a recipient of AAA's 4-Diamond Award for 1991, 1992, and 1993.

Moderate to expensive. Most dinners $13-23. Serving Sun.-Thurs. 5-8, Fri.-Sat. 5-9, Sun. brunch 10-2. Parking lot. Wheelchair accessible. Totally nonsmoking (except bar). Cocktail lounge. Children's menu. Reservations recommended. Dinner theatre Thurs.-Sun. Private parties (max. 280). All major credit cards. Checks OK with ID.

Stafne's Sunset Inn
Supper club / Steakhouse
2211 S. Hastings Way, Eau Claire / 715-832-1756

Stafne's has been serving fine food in Eau Claire since 1933, and has been under its present ownership since 1972. Most people come here for steaks, which are among the best in the region.

Inexpensive to moderate. Most dinners $7-12. Serving Sun. brunch 10-2, dinner 4:30-8:30. Weekdays lunch 11-2, dinner 4-9:30. Fri.-Sat. lunch 11-2, dinner 4-10:30. Parking lot. Wheelchair accessible. Smoking & nonsmoking sections. Cocktail lounge/bar. Children's menu. Seniors discount (age 60+). Reservations recommended. Local deliveries. Takeouts. Catering service. Private parties (max. 100). All major credit cards. Out-of-town checks OK with ID.

Sweetwater's Restaurant
American
1104 W. Clairemont Ave., Eau Claire / 715-834-5777
(2 mi N of I-94, on Hwy. 37)

Sweetwater's features American-style specialties such as fresh pasta dishes, oak-fired pizzas, almond-mandarin chicken salad, shrimp scampi, and slow-cooked prime ribs. Founded in 1985 by Larry and Nancy Williams, the restaurant has recently undergone extensive remodeling, enabling patrons to watch their foods being prepared. You'll find good variety and service here, at modest prices.

Inexpensive to moderate. Most dinners $8-12. Serving Sun.-Thurs. 11 am-10 pm, Fri.-Sat. 11-11. Parking lot. Wheelchair accessible. Smoking & nonsmoking sections. Cocktail lounge/bar. Children's menu. Reservations recommended. Local deliveries (charge). Takeouts. Private parties (max. 120). MC, VI, AE, Dis, DC. Out-of-town checks OK with ID.

Tally Ho
American
2703 Craig Rd., Eau Claire / 715-835-2211
(Take Exit #65 off I-94. Attached to Days Inn,
corner Hwy. 37 & Craig Rd.)

This is one of Eau Claire's largest convention centers, but the atmosphere at the Tally Ho is friendly, casual, and cozy. Specialties of the house include the Sunday brunch, the Friday night fish buffet, and char-grilled steaks anytime.

Inexpensive to moderate. Most dinners $7-12. Serving Sun. 7-2 & 5-9 (brunch 10-2), Mon.-Fri. 6:30-2 & 5-10, Sat. 7-2 & 5-10. Parking lot. Wheelchair accessible. Smoking & nonsmoking sections. Cocktail lounge/bar. Children's menu. Seniors discount (age 60+). Reservations recommended. Takeouts. Catering service. Private parties (max. 450). MC, VI, AE, Dis, DC. Out-of-town checks OK with ID.

★ ★ ★
The Creamery
American
Downsville / 715-664-8354
(From I-94, Exit #41A, S 10 mi on Hwy. 25, E 1/4 mi on Cty. C)

The Creamery is one of the finest restaurants in Wisconsin. Located in a turn-of-the-century creamery overlooking the Red Cedar River Valley, the building has been elegantly restored and the food is exceptional. All dishes are individually prepared. The menu ranges through beef, pork, chicken, shrimp, and fresh fish, with most dishes prepared with simplicity and all prepared with expertise. The sauces are superb, and there is a good wine list.

Moderate to expensive. Most dinners $10-17. Serving Tues.-Thurs. lunch 11:30 2, dinner 5-9, Fri.-Sat. until 10. Limited sandwich menu in off-hours. Sun. brunch 10-2, dinner 4:30-8. Closed Mon. *Closed Jan. thru Mar. 1994.* Parking lot. Wheelchair accessible. Smoking in cocktail lounge only. Limited children's menu. Reservations not accepted. Piano player in lounge Fri.-Sat. nights. No credit cards. Checks OK with ID.

Bolo Country Inn
Supper club
207 Pine Ave. W., Menomonie / 715-235-5596
(1 blk S of I-94 at Hwy. 25)

This popular supper club, set into seven acres of parklike grounds, has been run by the same family since 1957. There is an adjoining motel with a bed-and-breakfast atmosphere, and plenty of recreation nearby—golf, tennis, bike trails, and lakes. The restaurant gives horse and carriage rides on Friday and Saturday evenings. The Bolo offers a large menu of traditional supper club dishes, but is perhaps best known for its great steaks, all aged and cut in the Bolo's own kitchen. Another popular dish is the one-half pound platter of broiled shrimp.

Inexpensive to moderate. Most dinners $7-14. Serving Sun.-Thurs. 11-11, Fri. & Sat. 11 am-midnight. Parking lot. Wheelchair accessible. Smoking & nonsmoking sections. Cocktail lounge/bar. Children's portions. Special "early bird" prices. Reservations recommended. Takeouts. Private parties (max. 50). MC, VI, DC. Out-of-town checks OK with ID.

Norske Nook
Norwegian & Scandinavian cafe
207 W. Seventh St., Osseo / 715-597-3069
(Just off I-94, in downtown Osseo)

This little cafe in the little town of Osseo has received national attention and acclaim more than once. Yes, the food here is good (stuffed pork chops and Swiss steak are two popular platters), but the big attraction is the *pies!* Soon after the restaurant opened in 1974, word spread quickly about the sumptuous fruit and cream pies at the Norske Nook. Soon, travelers along I-94 were stopping by to take home whole pies. Word of mouth soon led to stories in big city newspapers and magazines, bringing in even more tourists. If Osseo were in a larger population area, it would be spoiled by the crowds. As it is, you can enjoy breakfast, lunch, dinner, and a wonderful piece of pie almost anytime. (I recommend sour cream-raisin, strawberry, or lemon meringue.)

Inexpensive. Most platters $4-5. Serving Mon.-Sat. 5:30 am-9:30 pm. Open Sun. in summer only, 8-4. Parking lot. Wheelchair accessible. Smoking & nonsmoking sections. No alcohol. Children's menu. No credit cards. Out-of-town checks OK with ID.

Harbor View Cafe
Scandinavian with garlic
First & Main St., Pepin / 715-442-3893
(Once you get to Pepin, you can't miss it)

If you ever find yourself wandering in summer along the Mississippi on Highway 35, make a real effort to pull off into the small town of Pepin, where you'll find a most wonderful cafe. The Harbor View, under the guidance of co-owner and head chef Paul K. Hinderle, serves up some wonderful fish dishes, including catfish baked in parchment, kedgeree (made from smoked grouper and salmon), and a fish stew that combines cockles, mussels, shrimp, squid, and other fish, all simmered in a saffron broth. There are also excellent pasta dishes, coq au vin, lamb, Scandinavian specialties (with garlic, of course), and more. The outstanding fresh fruit pies, French bread, and pastries are all made from scratch. The only bad thing about the Harbor View is that it's closed in winter, and usually very crowded in summer. But here's hoping you'll hit it just right. It's one to write home about.

Moderate to expensive. Most dinners $9-19. Serving *mid-May to mid-October*, lunch 11-2:30 Mon., Thurs., Fri., & Sat. Dinner 5-8 Mon., 5-9 Thurs. & Fri., 4:45-9 Sat., noon-7:30 Sun. Serving *mid-Oct. to Thanksgiving & mid-March to mid-May*, Fri., Sat., & Sun. only, same hours as above. *Closed Thanksgiving to mid-March.* Curb parking. Wheelchair accessible. Totally nonsmoking. Full bar. Children's menu. Reservations not accepted. No credit cards. Out-of-town checks OK with ID.

Index

Good Restaurants for Vegetarians

Outdoor Dining

Romantic Dining

Restaurants for Children's Birthday Parties

Restaurants for Dancing

Restaurants along I-90

Restaurants along U.S. Hwy. 43

Town & City Index

Restaurant Index